Roberta,

Smart Women
Smart Money
Smart Life

**Take Charge Now
To Have the Future You Deserve!**

Thank you for giving
my life renewed purpose!

by

Julia Anderson

Best ~Julia

Dedication

To my mother, Helen Rose, who shows me the way.

Julia Anderson

Preface

Would a reverse mortgage make sense for your elderly mother or someday, for you? Have you wondered about collecting Social Security benefits on an ex-spouse?

What about retirement? Does making the transition from full-time work to something new have you losing sleep?

Smart Women, Smart Money, Smart Life will help with answers to those questions and many more. Drawing on my years of reporting and writing about money, investing and financial planning, this book is anchored in authenticity. My goal: Give you a way forward when change hits you smack in the face.

Smart Women Smart Money, Smart Life is here to help you take charge of your financial future, manage transitions such as selling a business or re-investing your nest egg for the long-haul. It gives you how-to basics for challenges such as preventing financial abuse of an elderly aunt or getting out of a time-share contract.

Key book elements are drawn from my life experiences and those of my friends -- widowhood, divorce, leaving a full-time job, downsizing, traveling solo, aging parents. You name it, we've lived it. **And I've written about it.**

For me it began when I became abruptly 60 and single. It was a wrenching divorce much like sudden widowhood, but with the added twist of abandonment. Coming to terms with this reality wasn't easy. As a journalist and financial writer, I began digging into issues related to women and money.

It was a surprise to learn that women tend to ignore their financial futures, are less confident about investing, and often count on someone else to take care of long-range financial and estate planning. That's even though women typically outlive men.

The shocking fact is that half of American women 65 and older are single. Many are financially strapped, surviving on just Social Security. It doesn't have to be that way.

That's why I am passionate about financial literacy for women (and for the men in our lives.) I lead "money" workshops called **Own Your Future.** I write for women about money at my website *sixtyandsingle.com* and I host a public television series called **Smart Money** at TVCTV in Beaverton, Ore. where all aspects of saving, investing and money-management are discussed.

If you are looking for how-to tips about managing your nest egg, this book is for you. If you have experienced a wrenching loss like I did, this book can help. If you've wondered about writing a will, leaving a legacy or planning your end-of-life care, this book has answers. Are you newly single, on your own financially and wondering what's next like I was? This book will give you comfort and confidence.

You may face an unexpected "buyout" from your job or find yourself in financial crisis with an adult child. Your spouse may become seriously ill. This book offers a way forward.

While there may be losses in your later years, you also may find yourself joyfully remarrying as I did. Or celebrating new-found charitable work. Maybe you will find passionate renewal in a semi-retirement job. How about solo travel? Many women are hitting the road.

Smart Women, Smart Money, Smart Life gives you a road map to the future that you want and that you deserve. It's yours to plan and manage, now! - *Julia*

Acknowledgments

Each book chapter quotes experts – bankers, lawyers, financial planners, physicians among others -- on the topics discussed. I thank them ALL. Thanks also goes to my friends -- intelligent and caring women with diverse and dynamic lives. We have supported each other through trials and triumphs. Theirs are stories of resilience, of courage and power.

And thank you, Ken, the man I married my 64th year. It has been a great ride, literally, on his motorcycle. Who knew!

Julia Anderson

TABLE OF CONTENTS

Julia Anderson

MONEY

Julia Anderson

Looking Ahead: What's on Your Financial Horizon?

"Your past is not your potential.
In any hour you can choose to liberate the future."

--Marilyn Ferguson, American writer (1938-2008)

Women tell me that they don't think they have enough money saved for retirement. They say they never expect to stop working. With that they turn to other topics...out of sight, out of mind. And besides, they say, investing and managing finances is complicated. "I just can't get my brain around it," one friend said.

But it is not too late to plan and save for retirement -- even in your 50s or your 60s. It is not too late to learn how to manage money and, better yet, be an investor.

The trick is to stop ignoring your fuzzy financial future and get serious about long-term planning. Even if the news is not good, you at least will have a starting point.

National studies show how disconnected we are when it comes to long-range financial planning. Is it because women think they don't earn enough money to worry about it? What will be will be? Or are we just afraid? Fear can be paralyzing. Give yourself an hour to investigate the future.

Retirement planning before you stop working means working to align your expected income with your expected cost of living by reducing debt, cutting expenses and chucking as much money as possible into tax-deferred savings and investment accounts.

Don't expect any one else to do this for you. This is your life (single or married) and your money! And get ready --- many women in their 60s find themselves on their own because of divorce or the death of a spouse. How many of them wondered years earlier about what that would look like financially?

Some of my close 60-something friends are widowed. Others are caring for spouses with Parkinson's and life-threatening cancer. Among my single friends, one lost her house in the Great Recession. She now lives on a small pension after a life-time of teaching. Another in her late 60s is splitting with her husband after 40-plus years of marriage. The separation is his idea. She has not worked out of the house for most of that time. What will life on her own look like? She doesn't know.

News flash! Half of American women 65 and older are single and living on their own. Of those, 25 percent are living at or below the poverty line.

A long-range financial plan is the bedrock of a rewarding retirement. Why not become your own money "coach" to save and invest? Or ask a trusted friend for guidance. Hire a fee-based adviser. Think of it in terms of a diet: Set goals, check in regularly on your progress and celebrate your successes. Visualize the financial future you want. Then, step-by-step, get there.

FOR MORE:
Smart Women Don't Retire, They Break Free, by Gail Rentsch.
The Single Woman's Guide to Retirement, by Jan Cullinane
Suddenly Sixty, by Judith Viorst

11 THINGS I'D TELL MY
YOUNGER SELF ABOUT MONEY

"Only 47 percent of women are confident talking about money and investments with a professional."

--Fidelity Investments research in *How to Take Charge*

At 20, I understood the importance of saving and investing money, but there were other priorities – getting married, buying houses, having kids and establishing a household. I didn't get around to investing for the long-haul until my mid-30s. Even then, it was on again, off again. Things I wish I'd known sooner:

#1 - INVEST EARLY AND STICK WITH IT.

Sign up for your employer's 401(k) retirement savings program at the first opportunity. Put enough money into that account every year to at least get the employer's matching money. Don't be cautious. Invest this money in aggressive growth funds. Reinvest the dividends and embrace the miracle of compound interest/investing.

#2 - START AN INDIVIDUAL RETIREMENT ACCOUNT.

With $2,000 or less at some online brokerage firms you can start an IRA or a Roth IRA. Invest in low-cost index stock funds or buy a few individual blue-chip stocks that have a good track record and a good dividend. Reinvestment the dividends. Don't panic when stock prices or markets go into a downturn. You will end up managing your money in retirement; you might as well practice now.

#3 - CHECK MANAGEMENT & TRANSACTION FEES.

Experts say fees charged on your investment fund accounts are more important than what you are invested in because fees cut into reinvested earnings. High fees can result in hundreds of thousands of dollars less in your account at the end. Ask about management fees on your 401(k) funds. If you don't like what you learn (it should be 1 percent or less), start a separate IRA for yourself.

"Everyone talks about the benefits of compounding interest, but few mention the danger of compounding fees," says Kyle Ramsay, NerdWallet's head of investing and retirement.

#4 - AVOID DEBT.

Don't become house-poor or carry credit card debt. Taking on big debt limits your financial flexibility. Don't spend money you don't have on stuff you don't need. Debt is borrowing against your future income.

5 - BAD THINGS CAN HAPPEN TO GOOD PEOPLE.

Divorce, for instance. While you don't want or expect a divorce or the death of a spouse, it may happen. Women usually come out the losers in either case.

What to do? Set up an emergency fund. Buy inexpensive term life insurance on each other. Save for retirement as if you will be on your own.

If you divorce, be tough in negotiating your best possible financial future. "Every decision a woman makes after divorce, from where to live to how to increase her income, is an important part of this process." - LiveStrong.com.

6 - WRITE A WILL.

Even if you are young and in good health, a will spells out how you want your stuff dispersed if you die, and who you want to take care of your young children.

7 - DON'T BE SHY. ASK FOR PAY INCREASES.

If you are doing a good job and are a valued employee, your employer should be rewarding you with more money. More money means more goes into your 401(k) and you build a stronger employment record with Social Security. You have more options to save while still supporting your family. We are talking about receiving the same pay for the same job as your male counterparts.

8 - MAKE INVESTING ENJOYABLE AND REWARDING.

There are no mysteries here. The American free-enterprise system has created unbelievable wealth for average investors. Good publicly held companies report every quarter to their shareholders about how they are performing, they pay dividends every quarter. Set up an investment account and invest in things that you understand. Reinvest the dividends. Build your portfolio.

9 - DO NOT SNEER AT MONEY.

It's fashionable to say that money doesn't matter and that finding your passion is more important. Just make sure your dreams are financially reasonable. If you start your own business do you have the financial resources to stick it out? If you want to be a chef how will you pay the rent, save for the long-term? Money makes everything else possible.

#10 - UNDERSTAND SOCIAL SECURITY.

Set up an online account at *socialsecurity.gov* even if you are years from retiring. Track your annual wage reports. Those earnings are the basis of your benefits. Plan your employment glide path carefully in your 50s so that you don't have to take Social Security benefits too soon.

11 - UNDERSTAND THE DIFFERENCE BETWEEN SAVING AND INVESTING.

Saving is for hand-wringing people afraid to lose a penny. Investing is for people who understand the rewards of owning stock in good companies that offer share price growth AND pay a dividend. A certificate of deposit is safe but earning just 2% or 3% is only breaking even against inflation. Start investing early. Learn from your mistakes. Glory in your successes.

FACT: By investing $2,000 a year for 10 years starting at age 19, you can end up at age 65 with a whopping $2 million or more in a tax-deferred account, such as an IRA or 401k. That's thanks to reinvesting dividends and share value growth that together average 12% a year.

5 STEPS TO RETIREMENT PLANNING
WHILE STILL WORKING

*"You must gain control over your money
or the lack of it will forever control you."*

--Lydia Sweatt, Web producer at *success.com*

When I began writing about women and retirement, a friend of mine and I gave a series of workshops we called **5 Steps to Retirement Planning**. She was and is a CPA as well as an estate-planning attorney. At the time, she also was president of a regional chapter of the American Institute of Certified Public Accountants. The retirement planning steps below were gleaned from my conversations with her and from resources at the institute website. *www.aicpa.org*

STEP 1 - FIGURE YOUR NET WORTH

Knowing how much you are worth provides a marker in time for where you are financially and where you want to go. It provides incentive to do better. As you age into retirement your net worth should increase as you pay down debt and build your savings.

Net worth is the difference between what you own and what you owe. Net worth includes savings accounts, 401(k) holdings, bonds and money in CDs. There also are less-liquid assets such as cars, equity in your house and the jewelry that you inherited from grandma. Add up all those assets.

Then, subtract what you owe against that worth. (Your house mortgage, car loans, debts owed on credit card, and student loans.) The difference between what you own and what you owe is your net worth. FYI: According to GetRichSlowly.com, the average median net worth of U.S. families is $93,100.

HOW TO FIGURE YOUR NET WORTH

ADD UP THE VALUE of ALL YOUR ASSETS:

Savings account total   _____
Checking account total   _____
Retirement savings account(s)   _____
Individual Retirement account(s)   _____
Automobile(s)   _____
Market value of your house   _____
Jewelry   _____
Other valuables   _____
Furniture (if you had to sell it)   _____
Other   _____

TOTAL ASSETS   _____

ADD UP ALL YOUR DEBT:

Automobile loan(s)   _____
Home mortgage loan   _____
Student loan debt   _____
Personal loan(s)   _____
Credit card debt   _____
Other debt   _____

TOTAL DEBT   _____

NET WORTH: Subtract your total debt from your total assets

ASSETS   _____
DEBT   _____

NET WORTH   _____

As you age, your goal is to increase your net worth
by reducing debt, while saving and investing more.

STEP 2 - DETERMINE YOUR CURRENT HOUSEHOLD BUDGET

Maintaining a household budget is no small task when those cyber bargains are just a couple of mouse clicks away. But figuring out how much it is costing you to run a household -- pay rent, own a car, go on vacations, pay your power bill -- is worth knowing.

That's because until you know what you spend every month, you won't have a very good idea of where you might be able to cut costs and put that saved money into a retirement savings account.

Make a list of everything you are spending money on every month. Try not to create a miscellaneous category because that defeats the purpose of determining where your money goes.

The goal is to get a handle on your spending so that you can figure out what could change going forward.

Now add up your household income per month from wages, net business income or other sources. Are you spending every dime of income? Are there places you can cut to reduce your expenses? This current baseline cost-of-living budget will determine where you want to be down the road.

STEP 3 - SOCIAL SECURITY: CHECK YOUR BENEFIT OPTIONS

Visit the **Social Security Administration** website at *www.ssa.gov* and set up an online account using your Social Security number.

Calculate -- based on your work history -- what estimated benefits you will receive at age 62, at 66 and 70. You will learn that benefits increase by 8% for every year you delay taking them up to age 70.

But don't stop there because there are other ways to claim benefits based on your marital history, your age, and whether you are widowed or divorced.

For instance, you may be able to receive benefits on a spouse's Social Security account while letting your own account remain untouched. This can be complicated, but worth figuring out. Keep in mind that if you start benefits at 62 rather than at full retirement age of 66 or 67, your benefit amount will be permanently reduced up to 30%.

Schedule a face-to-face meeting with a Social Security rep at a local office to better understand your options for how and when to claim. Social Security is an important revenue stream for retirees and should carefully be planned.

STEP 4 – ESTIMATE OTHER RETIREMENT INCOME

What other sources of income will you have in retirement? Will you be tapping into a retirement savings account such as tax-deferred work-related 401(k) fund or a self-directed Individual Retirement Account?

How much do you plan to withdraw a year? 2%? 4%? What does that translate into in monthly (bill-paying) income?

Will you receive revenue from a rental property? How about a pension? Do you expect to inherit money or property from your parents or a great-aunt? Do you hope to ease into retirement by working part-time after you step away from the full-time job?

Consider these revenue streams to determine your annual and monthly income if you stop working at age 62, 67 or 70. Add this together with your estimated Social Security benefit (at those ages) and you'll have a better picture of your retirement income and how much you can withdraw annually from your nest egg. Will those resources last as long as you do?

STEP 5 - FIGURE YOUR BUDGET IN RETIREMENT

Put together an estimated retirement household expense budget like the current budget you have already formulated. Will your cost of living decrease in retirement? Or will it be pretty much the same as your current budget? Costs for such things as clothes and transportation likely will drop while those related to travel and medical expenses might increase.

THE BIG QUESTION: How does your estimated retirement cost-of-living budget match up with your estimated retirement income?

If retirement expenses outstrip your estimated retirement income, there is a lot you can do in your 50s to make things match up. For instance, could you keep working into your late 60s? Could you delay claiming Social Security benefits? Could you claim benefits on an ex-spouse before claiming them on your own account? Could you pay off your mortgage before you retire? Could you downsize to a smaller, less expensive place, or a different town?

These strategies can help stretch your retirement savings. And you'll have the information you need to form a plan and make changes, if needed.

If your estimated retirement income does NOT cover your estimated retirement expenses, you have two choices: Either aggressively save more money for retirement or reduce your living expenses before you retire to match your expected income.

And, if you're married, look at what your retirement income would be if your spouse dies. This is important for women because they often outlive their spouses.

EXPENSE AND INCOME WORKSHEET

U se the Expense and Income Worksheet on the following pages to calculate your current and future retirement needs. From all this, you may be surprised that retirement looks better than you thought. Or at least you'll know what you need to do before you can retire.

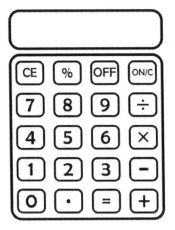

EXPENSE AND INCOME WORKSHEET

EXPENSES

SHELTER

Expense	Current, Monthly	In Retirement, Monthly
Rent/Mortgage		
Electricity/Gas/Water		
Garbage Removal		
Telephone/Internet		
Cable/Television		
Home/Apt Insurance		
Maintenance		
Property Tax		
TOTAL		

FOOD

Expense	Current, Monthly	In Retirement, Monthly
Groceries		
Dining Out		
TOTAL		

TRANSPORTATION

Expense	Current, Monthly	In Retirement, Monthly
Auto Loan or Lease Payment		
Gas		
Car Repairs/Maintenance		
Bus/Taxi/Uber, etc		
Auto Insurance		
Parking		
TOTAL		

CLOTHING

Expense	Current, Monthly	In Retirement, Monthly
Purchases		
Dry Cleaning/Laundry		
Alterations		
TOTAL		

INSURANCE

Expense	Current, Monthly	In Retirement, Monthly
Medical/Dental		
Life Insurance		
TOTAL		

HEALTH

Expense	Current, Monthly	In Retirement, Monthly
Medical Costs		
Dental Costs		
Pharmacy/Medications		
TOTAL		

OTHER

Expense	Current, Monthly	In Retirement, Monthly
Education		
Entertainment		
Personal Care/Haircuts		
Pet Expenses		
Dues/Subscriptions		
Charitable Contributions		
Other		
TOTAL		

INCOME

Source	Current, Monthly	In Retirement, Monthly
Salary		
Social Security		
Pension/401k/IRA		
Other Investment Income		
TOTAL		

EXPENSE AND INCOME COMPARISON

	Current, Monthly	In Retirement, Monthly
SUM OF ALL INCOME TOTALS		
Multiply by 12 for Annual	X 12	X 12
TOTAL ANNUAL INCOME		
SUM OF ALL EXPENSE TOTALS		
Multiply by 12 for Annual	X 12	X 12
TOTAL ANNUAL EXPENSES		
Subtract Total Expenses from Total Income	-	-
DIFFERENCE		

If your income exceeds your expenses, you're in good shape!
If your expenses exceed your income, something needs to change.

WHAT NEEDS TO CHANGE?

Julia Anderson

WHY DO WOMEN UNDERRATE THEMSELVES AS INVESTORS? FEAR!

"In order to rise above this fear, you need to be confident and comfortable in the moment and with yourself."

-- Lisa Haisha, creator of Transformative Therapy.

Women are more likely than men to underrate themselves when it comes to investing. Yet women usually oversee household budgets, are more willing to save for the long-term and are better bargain hunters. (See Wells Fargo Investment Institute study at *wellsfargo.com/investment-institute*).

So why do we feel uncomfortable when it comes to taking charge of our investments be they a 401(k) savings plan, an Individual Retirement Account or a retirement stock portfolio? Friends give me these reasons:

"I am just not interested...that's something my spouse takes care of."

"We like our financial guy...he seems to be doing a good job for us."

"When I met with my financial adviser, I thought we were on track. But I never asked questions."

"I feel over my head when it comes to the stock market, bonds. I'm clueless."

Yet most women over 60 will someday be financially on their own either from divorce or the death of a spouse.

Wells Fargo reports that women control $14 trillion of U.S. personal wealth and outlive men by an average of five years. They state the importance of women feeling comfortable with their investment decisions."

So, let's get comfortable with investing decisions before we find ourselves in a crisis.

Why not get involved now, take charge of your finances, and be ready for the future when you may need to manage on your own?

FOR MORE:
Sixtyandsingle.com
Feedthepig.org
360financialliteracy.org
American Institute of CPAs at aicpa.org

5 WAYS TO TAKE CHARGE OF YOUR INVESTMENTS

1 - ASK ABOUT 401(K) MANAGEMENT FEES.

If you are on the job, make sure you are getting the best performance from your 401(k) plan or Individual Retirement Account. Annual management fees should be 1 percent or lower. If retired and living on your nest egg, the same goes.

The goal is to make your money last as long as you do. Mutual fund management fees are a huge factor in how much you accumulate from compound reinvesting during your work life and how much your nest egg will keep earning during your later years.

2 - CHECK UP ON FINANCIAL ADVICE COSTS.

Are you are using a financial adviser to guide your investment strategy? Ask about upfront commissions on investment products or funds offered to you.

Anything more than a 1 percent fee or commission deserves a clear explanation. Why not go with dividend-paying individual stocks or low-cost index funds?

The reality is that most "managed" funds do not have the performance of a cheaper S&P 500 Index fund, but instead tend to have higher management costs and weaker performance. That's a big long-term negative. An annuity, for instance, may mean a fat commission for your broker.

#3 - BANISH YOUR INSECURITIES.

Investing is rewarding. Learn by doing. Wealth coach Deborah Owens, *deborahowens.com,* gives women an "F" when it comes to finances because of the myth that "financing and crunching numbers are too complicated." Owens encourages women to get beyond the fear and take a "calculated risk" with their money. Sitting on cash is not an investment strategy.

Get the most bang for the buck by improving your skills and investment knowledge, by asking questions about fees and commissions, and by not just hoping for the best. If you don't like your adviser, make a change. If a stock isn't doing well, sell it. Owens says, "Your ability to build wealth is directly related to your ability to take calculated risks." (Both now and during retirement.)

4 - BUILD A PORTFOLIO.

Set up an individual online investment account. Do the research. Start small. Use low-cost online brokerage firms. Put money into an S&P 500 stock index fund and/or a few blue-chip publicly traded companies with a stock dividend of about 3 percent. Reinvest the dividends.

Don't panic in a market downturn. The reinvested dividend money is buying more shares at a cheaper price! But keep an eye on business news and market trends. Over several quarters, a company's business profile may weaken. That may require adjustments. The goal is to balance risk with a record of performance over time.

Candace Bahr and Ginita Wall at *wife.org* encourage women to take on financial responsibility. They remind us that "**A Man is Not a Financial Plan**. In their **"Five Steps to Building a Portfolio,"** they recommend reading 'how to' books on saving and investing, using rating reports and staying up on financial news to gain confidence.

5 - GET REAL ABOUT RETIREMENT INCOME

Figure out where your income in retirement will come from. First, look at your Social Security account at *ssa.gov*. What are your benefits at 62, 66 or 70? What income will you have from tax-deferred retirement savings or investment income? Will you inherit money from your mother? Will you work longer to delay retirement, save more and increase your Social Security benefit? Can you catch-up by putting more money in your nest egg?

Answers to these questions will help you know where you stand and what you must do before quitting your job. The trick is to bring retirement household expenses in line with expected retirement income.

Plenty of women have made the transition from work to retirement. They are managing their money, staying within a budget, traveling, starting new relationships and getting the most from life. Taking charge of their finances is a key element of their confident future. It is **NEVER** too late!

FOR MORE:
  deborahowens.com
  wife.org
  wiserwomen.org
  ssa.org
  wellsfargo.com/investment-institute/

Julia Anderson

BUILD INVESTING CONFIDENCE:
A MUST FOR WOMEN

"Make the most of yourself by fanning the tiny, inner sparks of possibility into flames of achievement."

-- Golda Meir, Israeli stateswoman, Prime Minister
(1898-1978)

The easiest way to build investment confidence is by <u>doing</u>. Start an Individual Retirement Account with small cash infusions. Learn from mistakes and glory in the successes. Buy an individual stock, a stock fund or a bond fund.

Even though an employer may offer a 401(k) plan, gain confidence with your own IRA. That way when you roll over your nest egg into the IRA as you retire, you will know how to manage it. One of the most exciting times of my life was when at age 65, I redistributed my 401(k)-nest egg into the investments of my choice.

Here are four steps to gain investment confidence:

1 - LEARN BY DOING.

"Too often among my colleagues, advisers can be patronizing to women," a financial planner told me. "They can do things to their detriment. Women need to ask questions and get answers." Start your own investment portfolio. It doesn't take a lot of money. Reinvest the dividend money.

2 - FOLLOW YOUR INSTINCTS.

But do your research. If you don't understand an investment product, you should not put money into it. Buy what you know and like be it an individual stock in a company or a fund with a good track record.

3 - TRACK TRENDS BUT NOT EVERY DAY.

The news and analysis you find on 24/7 TV business news is (mostly) short-term. Don't be rattled by market ups and downs or speculative comments from talking heads. Take the time to read analysis from respected sources such as Forbes (*forbes.com*), the Wall Street Journal (*wsj.com*) or Bloomberg news or such online sites as *Fidelity.com* or Motley Fool (*fool.com*).

4 - UNDERSTAND THAT THINGS CHANGE.

At the end of the day remember that things can change. The fundamentals of an industry can change...look at the ups and downs of housing. Competition can increase, product quality can slip. These things can mean corporate revenue slips, earnings weaken, and the stock price may fall.

Ask yourself, is this temporary? Are the fundamentals of its business still strong? If so, hang in there. But if over several quarters things are getting worse, then take your lumps and sell. **Just as you go to your doctor for an annual check-up, do the same with your investment portfolio.**

More than anyone else, YOU care the most about your money. You must have the confidence to say this investment feels good, or this doesn't feel good when making your own decisions or when working with an investment adviser. Learn by doing.

WORKING?
INVEST IN AN IRA, NOT A 401(K)

"The main drawback of 401(k) plans is the lack of choices they offer. Since plans are controlled by your employer, you're limited to investing money in the funds your company chooses to offer."

--U.S. News & World Report Money

If you are working and worried about catching up on your retirement savings before the job runs out, start your own **Individual Retirement Account**. This is a particularly good idea if your employer is not contributing matching money to your work-related 401(k) retirement savings account or contributes very little – less than 6 percent at 50 cents to your $1.

What's the difference between a 401(k) and an IRA? They are both retirement savings plans that can generate significant savings over time through tax-deferment. (In the case of a traditional IRA, or a 401(k), or even tax-free in the case of a Roth IRA.)

Earnings inside 401(k)s and IRAs accumulate and can be reinvested without tax liability while you're working.

With a traditional IRA, you are required to start withdrawals at age 70 ½ whether or not you want to. With a Roth IRA, there's no withdrawal requirement.

With a 401(k), when your work life ends, your retirement savings typically roll over into an IRA that you will manage yourself or turn over to a financial planner to manage. So why not get some early practice by starting an IRA?

If possible, use both a self-directed IRA and a 401(k) to save. An IRA, says national financial-planning columnist, Scott Burns, "gives you freedom." You get the freedom to investment your IRA money where you want in anything from individual stocks to bond and stock index mutual funds.

The choices are far greater than with a 401(k) program usually offered through an outside money management firm as hired by your employer. And IRA management fees are typically less expensive.

Burns says, "Unless your employer offers a very low-cost plan combined with a substantial matching contribution, there is a good chance that you'll do better on your own."

So, let's say you're over 50 and playing catch-up on retirement savings. First make a household budget that you can live with. Stop giving money to your kids and grandkids. Cut back on the expensive vacations. Get serious about saving and investing for the long haul.

You've got a 401(k) at work. Keep putting money into it to receive whatever matching amount your employer is providing. Put half your 401(k) monies in stock mutual funds with good ratings and half in bonds...knowing that you're not taking anything out until at least age 66.

Consider setting up a Roth IRA. Why a Roth? Unlike a traditional IRA, contributions to a Roth IRA are not tax-deductible against current income, but later withdrawals are tax-free. (Not always and not without certain stipulations. For instance, the owner must be at least 59½ for tax free withdrawals on the growth portion above principal).

A Roth IRA offers fewer withdrawal restrictions and requirements. Transactions inside an account (including capital gains, dividends, and interest) do not incur a tax liability and there is no age requirement for withdrawals.

Contributions to a traditional IRA are tax-deductible but withdrawals are taxed as ordinary income later. Traditional IRAs require a minimum distribution at age 70½.

A low-cost IRA will likely beat any expensive 401(k) plan if there's no employer contribution.

How do you establish a self-directed Roth IRA or a traditional IRA? Set up an account with a brokerage firm --- the cheaper ones are online. Electronically transfer some money from your bank into the IRA account and watch it perform.

There are online investment sites that can accommodate your self-directed IRA account. Among them are *Vanguard.com, Fidelity.com, AllyBank.com, Schwab.com* and *eTrade.com*.

Brokerage firms and banks also offer IRAs, but fees are typically higher for buying and selling stocks, bonds and funds than with a self-directed online account.

By managing your own IRA, you get <u>crystal-clear clarity</u> regarding transaction fees and fund management fees and performance. Those things are difficult to ferret out with 401(k) funds despite more recent Congressional action requiring fee and expense disclosure. A lot is at stake.

FOR EXAMPLE: Columnist Scott Burns uses this comparison. Three 25-year-olds start putting $100 a month in 401(k) accounts. One account charges a nominal management fee of less than 1 percent. The others, respectively, charge 1 percent and 2 percent per year for fund management. All have a pre-tax annual return of 8 percent.

When the three retire (42 years later) at age 67,

- the less-than-1 percent fee account will have accumulated **$412,049**;

- the 1 percent fee account will have **$304,371;**

- and the 2 percent fee account will accumulate only **$227,016.**

This pretty much makes the case for checking into fees related to your 401(k) AND your IRA accounts. It's YOUR MONEY!!!   (And please, if you have daughters, encourage them to invest and save using a self-directed IRA now, even if they are not working. The longer the money can grow tax-free, the better.)

FUND MANAGEMENT FEES
MAY CRIPPLE YOUR RETIREMENT

"The average (American) wage earner stands to lose $109,407 over the lifetime of 401(k) retirement investing in fees and commissions that reduce the reinvestment factor in their savings programs."

-- Frontline in-depth report

Investigators at public television's *Frontline* produced a program called *"The Retirement Gamble"* in 2013 that created a firestorm of conversation and concern among those in the financial planning industry, retirement fund business, and those of us who advise and comment on the topic.

Key elements of Frontline's investigative report:

- Retirement money management is big business, generating billions for fund managers.

- Most retirees are unaware of the fees being taken out of their nest eggs that over time will cost them tens of thousands of dollars!

- Most companies provide their employees with limited choices for where their retirement money can be invested and despite recent Congressional action to bring more transparency to the business, the veil shrouding fund fee disclosure has not been lifted. The depressing news is that working Americans are being short-changed when it comes to 401(k) retirement management plans.

According to Frontline research, the average wage earner stands to lose $109,407 over the lifetime of retirement investing in fees and commissions that reduce their reinvestment factor.

Anyone who has spent time planning for retirement knows that to live comfortably without running out of money you will need a $1 million nest egg. Few of us will achieve that goal, but we're certainly not getting any help from the 401k industrial complex.

Tips from experts interviewed by Frontline:

- **Make friends with the people where you work who oversee managing the company 401k plan.** Ask them about fund choices and fund fees. Make this a mutually beneficial conversation. What fund manager is the company's plan using? Ask for full disclosure of management fees and trading fees. If you work at a larger company, go to brightscope.com to see fee rates.

- **Save as much as possible up to the 15 percent maximum limit in your 401k from day one.** If you're over 50, save even more in your 401k. Your minimum goal should be $1 million in your retirement nest egg by 65.

- **Don't invest in your own company's stock.** You're taking enough risk just by working there. Diversify your savings into low-cost index funds with expense ratios of 1 percent or less. What's an index fund? Index funds are a collective investment vehicle (fund) that aims to replicate the movement of an index of specific stocks or a set group of investments. For example, S&P 500 Index funds invest in the 500 leading publicly traded companies in the U.S. stock market. If the S&P 500 goes up, your S&P Index Fund will go up. No one is "managing" the fund and collecting a big fee for doing it. Get it!

If you leave a job don't be influenced by advisers who will push you into their own typically more expensive proprietary financial products. Either leave the money where it is or roll it into your new employer's 401k plan.

Start your own IRA!

That is easy to do with an online brokerage firm such as Fidelity, Vanguard or Charles Schwab where you are in charge and can monitor expense ratios on the funds you invest in at lower cost.

After reviewing the Frontline broadcast, Robert Brokamp of the Motley Fool wrote a piece called *"The Tyranny of the 401(k) Industrial Complex."* Brokamp summarizes by reminding us all that planning for retirement IS up to each one of us.

"However, you manage your finances, ensure yourself that it's doing more for your retirement than someone else's."

If the Frontline expose isn't enough, read Helaine Olen's book, *"Pound Foolish,"* an expose of the financial services industry. In it, Olen describes the business as a "world of illusionists, conjurers, and snake-oil salesmen of every stripe."

Again, who cares about your welfare, your retirement security and your money, more than you do? It's up to us all to get on top of our retirement planning, ask tough questions of our 401(k) fund managers and make sure we are not paying for someone else's retirement.

Julia Anderson

NEVER BORROW FROM YOUR 401(K).
HERE'S WHY.

"If you live for having it all,
what you have is never enough."

--Vicki Robin, American author of
Your Money or Your Life (1945 -)

A friend of mine, who recently retired from a management career in corporate human resources, said that time and again she saw women make a big financial mistake by taking money out of their 401(k) retirement savings plans.

"When you hit mid-life, say 20 to 25 years into your career, you may change jobs, there may be a crisis with an adult child. Or you might want to buy a new house," she said. "They see 401(k) money as an easy way to pay for what they think they need. But people forget the time-value of money. They steal from their future thinking that they can make up for it later."

Simply put: Borrowing from a long-term tax-deferred savings plan in mid-life can ruin your retirement by undermining the reinvestment growth potential of the account.

Take, for example, a single woman who enjoyed a high-paying career for 40 years. Every time she changed jobs, she took money out of her 401(k) during the transition to pay living expenses, buy a new car or go on a vacation. Now in her 70s, the woman is in ill-health and broke.

My friend said, "That $15,000 you saved from your latest job may not seem like a lot, but mid-career is when the miracle of compound interest/earnings begins to kick in. My advice to women – set-up a rainy-day savings account to get you through the rough patches. Roll your old 401(k) into an IRA. Never borrow money from your future."

She also recommends taking a hard look at your current lifestyle. "People think they need a certain standard of living but the reality is that we can live on a lot less," she said. "Living on less means more money goes into long-term savings and you are not tempted to borrow to pay for something you don't need."

Financial advice experts agree. Writers at MarketWatch.com list these reasons for why taking money out of a 401(k) is a bad idea:

- You are NOT saving when you borrow from a 401(k).
- Instead you are Losing Money. (Remember, money makes money)
- Time will work against you. Money left untouched in a 401(k)-investment portfolio will, on average, double every eight years.
- Meanwhile, if you can't repay the 401(k) loan, you are subject to a 10 percent early withdrawal penalty and subject to current income taxes.
- Borrowing from your 401(k) is a RED FLAG that you are living beyond your means.
- Borrowing from your 401(k) violates the golden rule of personal finance. PAY YOURSELF FIRST.
- You cannot make up a withdrawal.

An estimated 20 percent of Americans with a 401(k) exercise the borrowing option, reports the Employee Benefit Research Institute. The average loan is 11 percent of assets.

When I left a teaching job in my early 20s, I thought nothing of spending the measly $800 accumulated in my retirement account over the prior two years. That was 40 years ago. I could have left the money alone, added nothing more but reinvested the 10 percent annual earnings. The nest egg could have grown over the next 40 years to $36,207 of savings. From $800 to $36,207...not bad. Our 401(k)s do this on a grander scale!

While 401(k)s have come in for criticism, they remain the best way to save and invest for the long-term. It's not just saving but investing that will get you where you want to be. Stocks and bonds provide growth. Cash-only savings leaves you subject to inflation with not much return.

ADDITIONAL 401(K) MISTAKES

Many people fail to put enough money in a 401(k) to win employer matching money...that's free money that adds to the total. Meanwhile, make sure you and your employer understand what management fees are being charged on your 401(k) account. Higher-than-average fees eat into earnings.

While borrowing from your 401(k) can be a big mistake, trying to time the market by jumping in and out of investments can be equally harmful. **YOU CAN'T TIME THE MARKET.** Leave your investments alone, let them reinvest at bargain prices when markets are down. More shares mean more opportunity for growth when markets go back up.

If you change jobs, roll your "orphaned" 401(k) over into a single Individual Retirement Account set up through a brokerage firm. Most Americans have held 10 jobs by age 50 and 12 to 15 over a lifetime of work. "Too often, those orphaned accounts are frittered away in high-fee plans," say writers at Investopedia.com. "Properly invested into a single account, it becomes much easier to choose investments for a (diversified) portfolio that fits your long-term goals while keeping costs down."

Meanwhile, Congress may change some of the rules related to 401(k) to make it easier to borrow from those accounts by reducing the penalties for doing so. I don't get that. Americans already have a dismal retirement savings record. Why would we want to make it easier to undermine long-term savings to finance a life-style that we can't afford?

On the flip side, Congress also may make it easier for smaller employers to pool retirement savings money with a single state-verified retirement fund manager. Oregon is already under way with such a program called OregonSaves. Washington state is setting up the Washington Retirement Marketplace with the same goal.

Bottom line: Don't borrow from your 401(k). Avoid the need to borrow by having a separate rainy-day fund. Embrace compound growth of your 401(k).

FOR MORE:
  MarketWatch.com
  Bankrate.com
  myretirementpaycheck.org
  irs.gov   (Retirement Plan FAQS)

JOB BUYOUTS?
EARLY RETIREMENT OFFERS?
THE PROS AND CONS

"Don't make all your decisions based on your gut."

-- Scott Bishop, STA Wealth Management, Houston,
commenting on buyouts

Despite the growing economy, employers in certain industries continue to look for ways to cut costs by laying off workers.

Grocery giant, Kroger Co., cut costs by offering early retirement to 2,000 corporate administrative employees. Boeing Co. has used voluntary early retirement plans. Computer chipmaker, Intel Corp. cuts jobs. McDonald's is cutting middle management. Retailing is cutting jobs and closing stores.

In offering early retirement packages or job buyouts, employers are careful to avoid age discrimination. There are proven legal ways to do that. The early retirement package or buyout must be voluntary based on tenure or other neutral criteria.

A worker must get at least 21 days to consider the offer. Employees accepting an early retirement or buyout will be asked to sign a carefully drafted "release agreement" explaining their rights under federal law as they walk out the door. That makes it hard to later sue for discrimination.

So how do you evaluate an early retirement package if you find yourself in the cross hairs of your employer's cost reduction or buyout program?

There is much to consider: health insurance coverage after you leave the job, how close you are to age 65 when Medicare kicks in, when can you start taking Social Security benefits, if needed, and whether the company might offer "bridge money" to get you to Social Security.

The biggest decision comes first. What are the consequences of turning down the buyout offer, dodging the layoff bullet and keeping the job? Only your gut can answer that one. Your employer can't tell you.

There are a few positives. A layoff qualifies you for state **unemployment benefits** if you sign up and look for a new job through your local employment agency. Human resource administrators can explain how this works, what the job search requirements are and how many weeks you might be eligible for unemployment benefits.

Secondly, you can buy **health insurance coverage** through your former employer's insurance plan for at least 18 months, thanks to **COBRA,** a federal law passed by Congress in 1985. Some employers let you stay with the company health insurance plan until you reach 65 and qualify for Medicare.

In addition, some employers might offer **"bridging money"** to financially bridge the period between early retirement and when you are eligible for Social Security benefits.

But who wants to take reduced Social Security benefits at 62 when full benefits only kick in at age 66 or 67?

The biggest negative of taking an early retirement offer is that you no longer will have the job and its income to save through the company-sponsored 401(k). If there's a pension, it will likely be smaller than if you had kept the job longer. That means less money to live on in real retirement.

REINVENT YOURSELF

Some people reinvent themselves after an early buyout by starting their own business, by finding another job, or by working part-time. How long you have to figure that out depends on how much you employer offers in severance pay.

Severance usually consists of your current salary plus addition money for the number of years you've worked for the company.

Keep in mind that experts say that the amount of money you need to live on in retirement should by about eight times your income. So, if your household income is $100,000 a year, you will likely need $1 million (or more) in retirement savings to enjoy a modest retirement.

DON'T TAKE MONEY OUT OF YOUR 401(K)

Meanwhile, when leaving the job, do NOT make early withdrawals from your 401(k)-retirement savings plan. Just carefully move the money to a self-directed Individual Retirement Account with an online brokerage or a trusted local firm. Money withdrawn from a company-sponsored 401(k) or IRA is subject to a 10 percent "premature distribution" penalty before age 59½. Plus, you will pay federal income tax on the withdrawal. And you won't be growing that money for your real retirement.

Those who have been through an early retirement buyout will tell you that it is a stressful time with lots of ups and downs. It feels bad to be asked to leave a place where you like the job, like the contribution you make and enjoy the people you work with.

Financial planner Jim Blankenship writing in US News & World Report warns that **some companies "make an early retirement package seem more attractive than it really is."** He said that you may want to consult an independent professional adviser who "will work for your best interests" in negotiating a buyout.

Saying yes to a buyout may mean retraining for something new or doing something else that you've felt passionate about. Whatever, it will be a roller coaster ride.

SELLING YOUR BUSINESS?
IT TAKES A PLAN AND A TEAM.

"The brave may not live forever,
but the cautious do not live at all."

-- Richard Branson, business entrepreneur

M any successful enterprises were launched by people who have put their heart and soul into their business over the past 40 or 50 years.

What happens when it's time to move on, get out from under the daily grind of business ownership? Some just close their doors. Others sell to a new owner or let the kids carry on.

If you own a business, it is never too soon to start talking about succession planning with your kids or with younger employees who might want to take on operations when it is time for you to step-away.

"Those that work on a plan will have a much better chance of a hand-off," Ted Austin, senior vice president with the Private Client Reserve of U.S. Bank in Portland, told me.

According to industry statistics, 25 percent of family business transfers fail because of poor succession planning, he said.

"The biggest obstacle is around communication," he said. "Some people build a business with the idea someone will buy it. For others, the family name is on the door with the expectation the operation will stay in the family. One way or another you have got to talk about it."

For business succession planning to succeed, Ted Austin recommends these steps:

- Start talking sooner than later within the family about how to handle the legacy of your hard work.
- Find out if the next generation is interested in continuing the business or if you should begin considering a buyout by a group of employees or an outside investor.
- Set up a plan for how the transition will work. What's the timeline? How will responsibilities be shifted? Will dad and mom still come to work every day even though they may no longer be in charge? How will employees be kept in the loop?

Austin at U.S. Bank suggests that a good exit plan may spin out over a five- or ten-year period after a lot of questions have been answered. For instance, will it be a buyout by the children over time or will ownership shares be gifted to the next generation?

The more clarity in the plan related to legal governance of the business going forward means less stress during family gatherings at Christmas, or while on a family vacation in Bend. Austin cautions that mistrust or misunderstanding can put a damper on family events.

BUILD AN ADVISORY TEAM

Good succession planning means putting together a team of professional advisers – an attorney to write out a legal agreement, a financial planner to help with estate and retirement planning and a bank trust officer who can advise on tax strategies, creditor protection and asset management.

"Depending on the complexity, this professional help will cost money," Austin said. "Make sure the family understands that cost."

Succession planning evolves over time but doing it sooner than later can make the difference between a successful transition and disaster. Advisers at SCORE, a national small business mentoring network, say that business owners should not shy away from succession planning because it looks too far in to the future.

SCORE says that devising a formal plan that outlines who will own and operate the company, once you are not in the day-to-day role, is a critical path decision that has a direct impact on long-term business profitability.

The Small Business Administration recommends that before business owners embark on an exit strategy they should seek legal advice, and possibly a business evaluation expert who can help make sure every transition option has been considered.

Austin at US Bank in Portland says, "Without naming names, if you drive around the city you will see a lot of families that have built wealth, generation by generation, through a growing family business. Where it has gone extremely well, family members have been involved in the business. They have been able to look under the hood so that when the time comes they will be as ready as they can be. Or, they decide this isn't something they want to do, so everyone can plan for that change."

That business succession conversation must be launched by the business owner with the family.

Julia Anderson

HANDLING A WINDFALL:
IT'S EASY TO MAKE MISTAKES!

"I stand to inherit a lot from my father,
including high cholesterol and diabetes.
Oh, and maybe a few Beatles records."

-- Jarod Kintz, author and humorist, (1982 -)

A 60-something friend of mine received a $250,000 life insurance payout when her husband died from cancer a few years ago. She put the money in a bank savings account and has been sitting on it ever since, too scared to invest it.

She didn't realize that her money was losing value in that account because she wasn't putting it to work.

Inflation (the increasing cost of living) erodes cash savings at an average rate of 2 percent a year. Her $250,000 over five years would be worth $225,000 in buying power because of the rising cost of goods and services.

A windfall can come in many forms: An aunt leaves you unexpected money in her will. An employer offers you a lump sum pension buy-out. You settle a lawsuit. You win the lottery!

Coming into a large amount of money, especially if it is unexpected, may at first sound like a wonderful surprise. But, financial advisers say people often lose their heads when they see dollar signs.

They put the new money in a special category and go on a spending spree. Later they may have regrets about how the money was used.

For example, a middle-aged woman received $3 million in life-insurance money when her husband was killed in an on-the-job accident. She gave money to friends and family, took expensive trips, bought and sold houses and expensive cars. Within five years the $3 million was gone. She was back working as a nurse.

Coming into money can happen at any age, but women over age 50 will likely be among a large category of recipients. That's because they stand to inherit 70 percent of the assets that will be passed down over the next two generations. Those assets likely will come from their elderly 90-something mothers or when a spouse passes on. Or both.

"Whatever way it happens, coming into money has psychological implications," says Susan Bradley, author of *Sudden Money: Managing a Financial Windfall.*

"People think windfalls are about money. But it's really all about change and transition...and people need time to adjust," she says.

PLAN, IF YOU CAN

If you have the slightest hint that you might inherit money, make plans to avoid bad decisions. If it's a surprise, establish a money moratorium. Some say that you should not tell anyone of your windfall...not your kids, not friends.

Do nothing with your money for at least a few months, if not an entire year, advise the experts at *Bankrate.com.* Put it in safe place such as short-term bank CDs. Get it out of your checking account so you don't see it every day.

Seek the help of a therapist to sort through the emotional impact of your sudden wealth. Money changes who you are, affects relationships and may create resentments. "Everything a person has spent decades building changes in one fell swoop," says Dennis Pearne, psychologist and co-author of *The Challenges of Wealth.* He says, "Half the people who attain sudden riches spiral into self-destructive behaviors."

The advisers at *Fidelity.com* suggest that planning long-term is the best strategy. Set up an investment portfolio to reinvest earnings and income in 70 percent stocks and 30 percent bonds.

Walter Updegrave said in the Fidelity post, "Stick to low-cost choices like index funds or Energy Transfer Equities. (ETE) Half a percentage point a year in fees can boost the eventual size of your nest egg by 25 percent or more."

GET ADVICE

If your windfall is substantial, the experts recommend that you weather the storm by setting up a team of advisers whom you trust: a fee-based financial planner, an estate attorney and an accountant.

Don't ignore taxes. Some windfalls such as my friend's insurance payout are tax-free. However, a large inherited estate could be subject to federal and state taxes. Or if you cash out an inherited (and tax-deferred) individual retirement account you may owe taxes on the entire amount. How to handle these issues requires tax advice.

Don't quit your day job. Windfall recipients often under-estimate how much money they'll need to replace their income, says William Hammer in the Kiplinger Personal Finance newsletter. "If you earn $50,000 a year, you'll need to invest anywhere from $1 million to $1.5 million to generate enough to replace that income, he said. Those who are retiring already know this from calculating how much they can withdraw from their 401(k) nest eggs.

Geoff Williams, writing for *usnews.com* says getting rich can be easy compared to staying rich. "Do nothing for as long as possible," he says. "Don't spend unusually large amounts of money. The last thing you want to do is blunder into an expensive purchase you can't return and will soon regret," he says. Issues worth thinking about include your current debt, your plans for retirement and taxes.

WET BLANKETS

The experts throw wet blankets on having fun with your new-found money. But at least one suggested a "small splurge" on say, a trip you've always wanted to take. "A small indulgence could reduce the chance that you'll blow your entire windfall," said Mitch Brill, a certified financial planner (CFP) with MassMutual Financial Group.

Let's face it, a windfall will likely only come around once in a lifetime, so give yourself time to figure out how to make it last a lifetime. As for my friend, she finally moved her insurance money into a S&P 500 Stock Index fund that with earnings and share price increases should generate 8 to 12 percent in average annual earnings. That money gets reinvested to build her nest egg. Better late than never.

DEFINITION: WINDFALL – noun.
An unexpected, unearned or sudden gain or advantage usually to do with money. The English word windfall originates from the Middles Ages when royalty or lords owned most land and estates and serfs were forbidden to pick fruit or fell a tree. However, if a storm or strong wind blew down a tree, it was referred to as a "windfall" and free for the taking.

FOR MORE:
"Handling a windfall," *sixtyansingle.com*
"What to do with a windfall," *fidelity.com*
"Four Steps to Protect a Windfall," *bankrate.com*

Managing Your Nest Egg

You have worked for 30 years while raising kids, making mortgage payments and saving for the long-term. In your 60s that comfortable rhythm of life begins to change.

At 60, you will probably still be working full-time but by the time you reach 70, you have likely left the big job.

Along the way, you've signed up for Social Security benefits, have a Medicare card and are buying additional health insurance coverage. If you're lucky, the changes will be gradual.

Maybe you will continue to work as a consultant or freelancer or take a part-time job to save more and hold off taking Social Security until 70.

Your 90-something mother may enter a care center, then pass on. You inherit her assets.

In your 60s you don't think about losing a spouse, but it happens. Four of my friends are on their own after losing husbands to cancer. Two others divorced.

Your financial profile will change. Even with Medicare, you likely will spend more on health care and additional health care insurance coverage. During your "active retirement" years, travel may be important.

Julia Anderson

COLLECTING SOCIAL SECURITY
ON AN EX-SPOUSE?

(IT'S BETTER IF THEY'RE DEAD)

"Social Security isn't a Ponzi scheme.
It's not bankrupting us. It's not an outrage.
It is working."

-- Rachel Maddow, political commentator, author. (1973 -).

The Social Security Administration has a provision that allows Americans to claim benefits on an ex-spouse's account if they were married to that person for 10 years or more. That's straightforward but sorting out the details from there gets confusing.

Questions about ex-spouse benefits are a hot topic. But your financial adviser may not give you accurate information or know how you can claim these benefits. Neither will your best friend.

Getting the right answers about Social Security will require a face-to-face session with someone at your local Social Security office to find out how the rules apply to you.

Call **800-772-1213** to set up a local appointment.

You will learn that collecting benefits on an ex-spouse works best if you are 62 or older and single or that your ex-spouse is dead.

If he's not dead, it is better to wait until your own full-retirement age (66 or 67), then collect on his account. Collect on your own account at age 70 at a higher monthly pay-out rate.

Here are several scenarios for how Social Security spousal rules apply:

SCENARIO # 1: YOUR EX-SPOUSE IS LIVING AND HAS RE-MARRIED.

First, you CANNOT be re-married and collect on your living ex-spouse's account before your full retirement age. Next, you CAN NOT collect on a spousal account unless you are at least 62 years old (minimum retirement age). There are exceptions if you are caring for a child under age 16 of your ex-spouse.

Further, according to Alan Edwards with the Social Security Administration in Portland, Ore. your ex-spouse must either be receiving benefits, or entitled to receive them. And finally, if you are less than 'full retirement age' you must file for benefits based on your own employment. (NOT your ex-spouse's.)

SCENARIO # 2: YOUR EX-SPOUSE IS DECEASED.

If you were married more than 10 years to an ex-spouse who is dead, no problem. You CAN take survivor benefits on his account before your full-retirement age. Reduced survivor benefits are payable at age 60 or as early as age 50 if you (the survivor) are disabled.

For women, this can be a big benefit. It's a way to gain retirement income without tapping their own Social Security account until their higher full retirement age or up to age 70. It's a way to take advantage of "delayed retirement credits." You may also remarry after age 60 and keep the survivor's benefit.

SCENARIO # 3: YOU'VE ALREADY CLAIMED BENEFITS ON YOUR ACCOUNT.

If you have started taking Social Security benefits on your own account and an ex-spouse dies, go back and talk to Social Security. The rules change.

You may then be eligible to file a claim on that account before your own full-retirement age. Even if you've been collecting on your own account, you may be able to switch to the spousal account.

SCENARIO # 4: YOU'VE REMARRIED, BUT YOUR CURRENT HUSBAND DIES.

Everything changes if you are married and your current spouse dies. You only must be married to this person for nine months to claim Social Security benefits on his account. There are some exceptions to this rule related to a traumatic or accidental death.

Having spent some time at *socialsecurity.gov,* I can say the agency's website is generally easy to navigate. But, on the topic of spousal benefits, ferreting out the information is a challenge. This is an area of confusion for many women.

MAKE AN APPOINTMENT

If you are 60 or over, single, and wondering or worrying about what you might be able to claim on an ex-spouse's account, don't wait. Find out in person where you stand and learn what your benefit options are from a Social Security Administration expert. For answers or to set up an appointment, call **Social Security's toll-free number at 800-772-1213.**

Every case is different. What you may have heard from a friend or from a financial adviser, or have read, may not be up-to-date or accurate. Not even all Social Security reps have all the answers, so you might want to make two appointments. Then, compare notes. There are a couple of thousand ways to collect Social Security depending on age, marital status and work history. Take your time to sort it out.

FOR MORE:
Social Security Administration, "What Every Woman Should Know" pamphlet.
Bankrate.com, "Ex-spouses and Social Security."

Julia Anderson

INFLATION CAN EAT UP YOUR RETIREMENT. PLAN AHEAD!

"Inflation is when you pay $15 for the $10 haircut you used to get for $5 when you had hair."

-- Sam Ewing, former professional baseball player. (1949 -)

The nation's Consumer Price Index typically increases 2 percent a year. That means a market basket full of consumer goods and services – housing, food, energy -- that cost $100 in 1982-84, now costs $240.

Until lately, inflation has not been a worry with bank interest rates much below average and the economy is low gear. Now, we must take inflation more seriously because the rising cost of living will eat into our retirement household budget.

(What is inflation? It is a rise in the general level of prices of goods and services in an economy over time.)

That said, the costs of certain items within the Consumer Price Index (CPI) are increasing at a faster rate than the overall annual 2 percent upward trend.

Medical costs for everything from doctor and dentist visits, to drug costs, nursing home fees and hospital charges jumped 5.1 percent last year. Housing costs, up 5 percent.

If you will be living on a fixed retirement income, the rising cost of living will be a negative. Ronald Reagan called inflation as "deadly as a hit man."

For example: If you have a $60,000-a-year lifestyle, a 3 percent annual inflation rate will require $80,635 of income in 10 years and $120,000 a year in 20 years to stay even.

It might be worse. During some periods of the past 50 years, annual inflation has skyrocketed as much as 10 percent in one year.

COPING WITH INFLATION

1. **Consider investing in TIPS** (Treasury Inflation Protected Securities). The principal investment in a TIPS bond increases with inflation and decreases with deflation, as measured by the Consumer Price Index. When a TIPS bond matures, you are paid the adjusted principal or original principal, whichever is greater. What's more, TIPS pay interest twice a year at a fixed rate. To learn more, visit **TreasuryDirect.gov.**

2. **Look at an immediate income annuity** with an inflation rider. Income annuities are insurance contracts purchased with a single lump sum of cash that offer immediate income payments (usually monthly) for a specified period or for the annuitant's lifetime. Do your homework on annuities. Get a second opinion before handing over a chunk of your savings. Financial advisers usually receive a big upfront commission on the sale contract. So, get outside advice on what you're buying and if this is a good idea.

3. **Consider a variable annuity with a guaranteed accumulation rider.** This type of rider guarantees that the minimum amount received by the annuitant (you) after the accumulation period, or a set time, is either the amount invested or is locked-in gain. This rider protects you from market fluctuations. Find out more at *sec.gov*. On the plus side, guaranteed annuity payments provide income. But, there are pitfalls.

4. **Delay taking Social Security.** Among the best ways to address the risk of inflation is to delay your Social Security benefits, if possible, until age 70. Doing so, means you get the highest possible, inflation-adjusted, guaranteed stream of income from Social Security. The annual benefit increases about 8 percent per year until you are 70.

Meanwhile, that $50,000 in cash savings you have stashed at the bank is losing value to the tune of $1,000 a year thanks to inflation. It will take that much more money (2 percent of $50,000) next year to buy the same stuff. Keeping too much cash around even in troubling economic times is costing you money.

> **Consumer warning from the FDIC:**
> It's important to remember that some annuities may lose value. These products are not insured by the FDIC or the FDIC-insured banks or saving institutions that offer them.

Julia Anderson

MAKE YOUR NEST EGG LAST.
MANAGE YOUR INVESTMENT MIX.

"Bankers know that history is inflationary,
and that money is the last thing a wise man will hoard."

--William Durant, industrialist. (1861-1947)

Women often wait until their early 50s before thinking about retirement. How much can we save? Will our nest egg last as long as we do? How much time do we have? Lots of questions but few answers.

In our changing economic environment with interest rates increasing, stock markets in flux and bond options confusing, many of us turn to experts. Here are two scenarios from the experts for how to manage your nest egg in retirement.

SCENARIO # 1: STICK WITH STOCKS

"With a $1 million 80/20 stock-bond portfolio mix, you have only a 14 percent chance of running out of money before you die."
- New York Times

Conventional financial wisdom has people getting more conservative with their savings nest egg as they near retirement. This formula has two parts---save like hell over your lifetime of work, then put the money in a safe place and live on it the rest of your retired life. **This plan means that many of us will run out of money before we die.**

Safe places touted by financial advisers include bonds, bond funds, money market funds, certificates of deposit. Only a small portion of your savings should be exposed to the vagaries of stock markets or "risky investments" in individual publicly owned companies, they say.

But experts say an 80 percent stock and 20 percent bond portfolio mix will get you a lot farther down the financial road than what conservative advisers are recommending. The trick is to keep making money with your nest egg even as you spend it.

Old thinking has your nest egg going into tax-free municipal bond funds with an annual withdrawal rate of 4 percent. A $1 million investment would produce about $40,000 of income a year. There are problems with this plan, say experts at the New York Times.

The newspaper's research shows that a couple using this plan for their $1 million nest egg has a shocking 72-percent probability of running through their bond portfolio nest egg before they die.

"The probabilities are remarkably grim for retirees who insist on holding only bonds in the belief that they are safe," Seth Masters, chief investment officer of New York-based Bernstein Global Wealth Management told the Times.

The fundamental problem as explained in the Times article: With bond funds earning below 4 percent a year, you can't withdraw 4 percent a year without depleting that portfolio over time. Add in an average 2 percent-a-year inflation rate and you're up against it.

There's another challenge -- we're living longer. We all know people over age 90. My mother died at 98. Most of the people in her assisted-living center were over 90.

According to the Social Security Administration, the average 65-year-old woman today can expect to live to 86. One out of 10 people (women and men) who are 65 today will live past 95.

Meanwhile, the assets we may have accumulated over a life time may not be nearly enough to sustain us into old age. According to the Times research, only 8.1 percent of Americans have a net worth of $1 million or more (excluding home equity value). Even with $1 million it will be tough to not outlive our money.

HOW TO COPE?

Consider putting 80 percent of your nest egg into stocks or stock mutual funds and only 20 percent in bonds, say the experts. An 80/20 mix of stocks and bonds with an annual withdrawal rate of 4 percent will reduce the probability of running out of money to just 14 percent. With a 3 percent withdrawal rate the probability drops to just 4 percent.

Yes, stocks are higher risk but in our new world, so are bonds. Stocks pay dividends and have typically increased in total value over time.

Keep enough cash in your accounts to weather a market downturn while leaving the rest in equities where quarterly dividends are reinvested.

If you read Burton Malkiel's *"A Random Walk Down Wall Street"*, or Peter Lynch's *"One Up on Wall Street"*, you will learn that stocks over the long-term outperform bonds.

There are two ways to benefit from stocks -- the dividend they pay quarterly on shares you own in a company and by an increase in share value over time as the company grows and adds to its balance sheet.

Investing in a no-load S&P 500 index fund offers these rewards at relatively low cost and low risk since your investment money is spread over the 500 largest U.S.-based publicly held corporations. Management fees are typically 1 percent a year or less. Stick with stocks.

SCENARIO # 2: START WITH BONDS, MOVE SLOWLY INTO STOCKS

Until lately, financial advisers have shared two long-standing rules:

Rule # 1: You can safely withdraw 4 percent of your nest egg retirement savings each year without running out of money in the long-run.

Rule # 2: When reinvesting retirement funds start with riskier assets and move into safer bonds as you age. But, right now (2018), both stocks and bonds are expensive by historical standards and in some danger of losing value.

THERE ARE <u>NEW RULES</u>:

The new withdrawal rule: <u>3 percent is the new 4 percent</u>. In other words, withdraw 3 percent from of your portfolio a year instead of 4 percent.

Experts at the American College of Financial Services say that 3 percent is a safer withdrawal rate. A lower withdrawal rate means more money stays in your portfolio and continues to earn income to be reinvested for the long-term.

Let's look at some numbers:

You have $1 million in retirement savings:

A 4 percent withdrawal rate = $40,000 a year.

A 3 percent withdrawal rate = $30,000 a year.

You have $500,000 in retirement savings:

A 4 percent withdrawal rate = $20,000 a year

A 3 percent withdrawal rate = $15,000 a year.

Can you live on $30,000 a year, plus your Social Security benefit? Many people are living on less. Can you live on $15,000 or $20,000 a year, plus Social Security?

WHAT TO DO?

The new thinking has retirees reducing stock exposure in the early years of retirement to protect against market declines, which are more likely at the end of this long bull market that we've enjoyed. Then gradually moving back into stocks as they age.

If a BEAR MARKET occurs in the early years of retirement, a stock-heavy portfolio might never recover if you must sell stock at a depressed price during a downturn.

In a bear market, bonds (even at today's higher values) will do better and offer less risk.

TO REVIEW:

When planning for retirement, make your income calculations based on a 3 percent withdrawal rate rather than the traditional 4 percent to allow more of your portfolio to grow and last longer.

Secondly, consider starting your retirement with more of your portfolio invested in safer bonds, rather than stocks, and gradually move into stocks as you age.

The idea is to stretch your retirement nest egg the estimated 28 years you may live in retirement.

If this scares you, talk to a financial adviser about your retirement income options, read up on investment strategies for withdrawing from your nest egg. Make sure you understand the underlying risks of bonds in an environment that has the Federal Reserve Bank raising interest rates.

And remember that if you are in good health at age 65, you will likely live into your mid- to late-80s. And we all know people living into their 90s.

FOR MORE:
"Why You Should Hire a Financial Planner, even if You're Not Rich," NY Times
"Forget the 4 % Rule," Wall Street Journal
"How Much Can You Withdraw in Retirement?" – *balance.com*
"How can I Make my Savings Last?" – *fidelity.com*
"How Much should you withdraw from your Retirement Savings each year? " - Motley Fool at *fool.com*

WARREN BUFFET ON
MANAGING RETIREMENT MONEY

"I've never delayed an investment decision
because of what might happen in Washington D.C."

-- Warren Buffett, investor, (1930 -   )

A re you sticking with the U.S. economy? Warren Buffet is. Not long ago, we were coming out of a dark tunnel -- the worst economic downturn of the past 50 years. Terrible timing it would seem for rolling a 401(k) nest egg into a self-directed Individual Retirement Account, right? Not so.

For me it was a great time to move my accumulated tax-deferred savings from 26 years of full-time newspaper work into an IRA. I put it all in the American stock market and more than doubled the value of my investments over the next eight years.

Do I expect the same performance going into the next eight years? No. With economic recovery well under way, inflation is heating up, interest rates are going up and stock market growth is slowing.

Nevertheless, I say thanks to Wall Street, our free-market system and the enterprising American corporations that have made my financial future a lot brighter.

Using a self-directed online brokerage firm, I moved my savings into a combination of stock index funds and individual corporate shares.

When I left the full-time job, I was excited to take charge of my nest egg.

Savvy friends advised me on investing strategies. I read investment advice books, I followed financial news and continued to use my mother as a role model for good investing habits.

She liked buying stock in individual companies that paid a good dividend, which she then reinvested in more company stock every quarter.

So, despite the dysfunction of Congress, despite the federal debt, despite Europe's on and off struggle with EU monetary issues and the drumbeat of negative news from the Middle East and North Korea, my investments are performing well.

Like ace investor Warren Buffett, I am sticking with large-cap U.S. corporations that show good quarter-to-quarter performance and that pay a decent dividend (somewhere above the current 2 percent inflation rate).

WARREN'S PHILOSOPHY:

The best (investment) opportunity is the United States of America where great corporations and businesses operate within the rule of law, where we are blessed with exceptional natural and human resources and where our regulated capitalist society creates new ideas and new opportunities.

Meanwhile, the European Union struggles with bureaucratic dysfunction and socialist leanings while Asia contends with corruption and red tape.

Most large U.S. corporations do business in these markets anyway, so if things begin to look better off-shore, American businesses will benefit from those global operations.

In times of high anxiety, I turn to Warren Buffett who reemphasizes the importance of being a long-term investor.

It turns out that markets perform just about the same (up an average of 11.5 percent a year) under Republicans as under Democrats.

Buffett sees steady improvement in the U.S. economy and that 2 percent-a-year growth with less than 1 percent of population gain means 1 percent of "real growth per capita."

In 20 years, he said, that's 20 percent of real economic expansion. "If every generation lives 20 percent better than the generation before them, that's not terrible," he said.

FOR MORE:
"One up on Wall Street," by Peter Lynch
"A Random Walk Down Wall Street," by Burton Malkiel
"Investing 101: Making Your Money Work for You,"
thebalance.com
"Our Guide to Investing for Beginners," The Motley Fool,
fool.com/retirement
"Chicken Little Investing," by Ginita Wall at wife.org
Ellevest.com
Investopedia.com
SmartAsset.com
thepennyhoarder.com

Julia Anderson

How to Hire (or Change) a Financial Adviser.

"Better to trust the man who is frequently in error than the one who is never in doubt."

-- Eric Sevareid, CBS news commentator (1912-1992)

Studies show that women, while good at budgeting, bill paying, and saving, may be less confident when it comes to investing and managing long-term savings.

Let's say you are leaving your full-time job and taking your 401(k)-nest egg with you. Are you going to manage it yourself or will you turn to a professional?

If you want professional advice, here are questions to ask a financial planner/adviser before giving them your life savings. Treat this process like a homework project and don't be uncomfortable asking the uncomfortable questions. It's your money, your future and your retirement.

QUESTIONS TO ASK WHEN CHOOSING A FINANCIAL ADVISER:

- How do you get paid? A commission on product sales, fee per transaction, or both?
- Can you manage my assets for a 1 percent or less management fee?
- What's your background and experience?
- What's the strength of the company you work for?
- What do your clients say about you? Ask for references.
- What are your checks and balances?
- Will you put your proposals in writing?

- What are the potential pitfalls of the investment products you are offering?

- What do other professionals say about you?

- Ask yourself what your gut-level comfort is with this adviser?

- Ask yourself, when you meet with your adviser do you come away feeling good about what you've learned, where you're headed?

Don't hire or continue to use a financial adviser just because they are nice!!!

Do the math at least a couple of times a year. How are your investments doing in comparison to the S&P 500? If the S&P is up by 15 percent and your holdings are up only 7 percent, then ask tough questions about why the weak performance? You might do better on your own or by switching advisers.

MEDICARE:
DO YOUR HOMEWORK WHEN
BUYING ADDITIONAL COVERAGE

*"Social Security's not the hard one to solve.
Medicare...that is the gorilla in the room..."*

-- Joe Biden, former U.S. Vice President. (1942-)

Medicare....it's what you sign up for at age 65, like it or not, working or retired.

Signing up is easy. The hard part is buying additional health insurance coverage because Medicare doesn't cut it when it comes to keeping you out of the poor house if you have a major health problem.

STEP 1: Sign up for Medicare through the Social Security Administration at *ssa.gov*. You have a three-month window on either side of your 65th birthday to sign up. Failure to do this means penalties. Once signed up, you get a Medicare card.

There are four parts to the Medicare program:

A. Hospital Insurance - helps pay for inpatient care in a hospital or skilled nursing facility (following a hospital stay), some home health care and hospice care.

B. Medical Insurance - helps pay for doctors' services and many other medical services and supplies that are not covered by hospital insurance.

C. Medicare Advantage - plans are available in many areas. People with Medicare Parts A and B can choose to receive all their health care services through one of these provider organizations under Part C.

D. Prescription Drug Coverage - helps pay for medications doctors prescribe for treatment. Go to ssa.gov for a basic helpful Medicare overview.

STEP 2: Medicare-only or something more? Decide if you will go with just Medicare coverage or whether you can afford to buy additional coverage through a Medicare Advantage or a Medigap plan that broadens coverages and care options.

Most people want more than the minimum Medicare program. Your provider will also like you better if you've got an additional plan. Providers lose money on Medicare-only patients since the federal government only pays 50 cents to 80 cents or less for every $1 of care provided.

STEP 3: Call the business office of your primary care provider and ask what Medicare advantage/Medigap plans your provider accepts. Providers aren't supposed to recommend plans but they can tell you what they accept. Their answers will save you time and help you cut through all the junk mail.

(Warning: If you are relocating to another city, many providers will NOT accept new Medicare-only patients. They usually will accept Medicare-Advantage or Medigap patients.)

Don't be buffaloed by all the marketing scare tactics that arrive your mail box. In fact, ignore all that stuff. Stay local or at least regional in selecting coverages.

STEP 4: Check out Advantage plans and Medigap plans. Because I want better coverage and I also want added dental and vision coverage, I went with a Medicare Advantage plan. Many providers will recommend an insurance broker to help you sort through coverage options and costs.

Some clinics offer free weekly Medicare classes to explain the process and options. Once you've selected an insurance provider, call them. Have them walk through their various packages, levels of coverage and related costs. Pick the one that best suits your needs. If you are in good health and use few if any medications, a cheaper Medicare Advantage plan is probably the best choice. In a year, if you don't like the plan you can change it.

STEP 5: Figure the budget impact. Before signing up, figure the cost. If you are collecting Social Security benefits, the agency will start withholding money from your monthly benefit check once you hit 65 to pay for Medicare. If you're working, you must sign up for some combination of Medicare and additional insurance coverage through your employer.

FOR MORE:
Medicare.gov
"Understanding Medicare" at aarp.org/health/medicare

Julia Anderson

Taking Care of Business

DOWNSIZING, FRANCHISE OWNERSHIP, REVERSE MORTGAGES, TIMESHARE CONTRACTS

"I'd say less than 10 percent of prospective franchisees consult an attorney (franchise or otherwise) before signing a franchise agreement."

– Kevin B. Murphy, franchise attorney and author of *"The Franchise Investor's Handbook."*

BUYING A FRANCHISE?
BEWARE! THERE ARE DOWNSIDES!

M any people are looking for new business opportunities in their semi-retirement -- something challenging that will keep them busy and generate income.

Buying a franchise business is an option. But before you write a big check out of your life savings, make sure you understand all aspects of the deal and the obstacles you may face in an over-saturated industry.

Franchising in America in the past 60 years has allowed many good ideas to grow into big businesses while generating handsome returns for the founder and franchise partners. About one in 10 Americans work for a franchise-chain operation.

The franchise formula: Franchisers have a great idea or concept but can't afford to expand the business idea on their own. Instead they offer the concept to franchisees, provide the training, marketing and ongoing support to open franchisee stores or other business. In turn, the franchisee invests his/her own money to buy into the franchise corporation, then sets up the business to operate within the framework of the franchise rules.

Kevin B. Murphy, a San Francisco attorney and expert on franchising, operates an informative website worth visiting called *franchisefoundations.com.* Murphy recommends that anyone looking at a franchise business opportunity consider these issues:

INDUSTRY TRENDS

Industry Trends - Is the franchise in a cutting-edge industry that is doing well currently and is projected to do well in the future despite any economic slowdown? Education, health care and home-improvement services are stable categories. Food is over-saturated generally and, except in exceptional circumstances, is not worth the high investment, long hours, headaches and marginal income, Kevin Murphy says.

TOTAL INITIAL FRANCHISE INVESTMENT

In general, don't expect a franchise that requires a five-figure initial franchise investment to produce a six-figure income. As with most things in life, you get what you pay for. On the other hand, don't assume a six-figure investment will lead to a six-figure income level. Be realistic and conservative.

REAL BUSINESS CREDIBILITY

Is this a legitimate retail business, as opposed to a "work out of your home" operation? The majority of work from home concepts produce marginal income at best, he says.

FRANCHISE MANAGEMENT EXPERTISE

Does the management team of the franchiser (the company selling you the franchise) have executives with demonstrated past achievement and experience in operating a franchise company? If not, this is a big red flag.

In other words, can you trust this franchiser to make sure franchisees are successful?

(Read, Josh Kosman's book, *"The Buyout of America,"* about how private equity firms are raiding America's franchise industry, ruining businesses and shafting franchise store owners.)

The federal **Small Business Administration** offers plenty of franchise-buying information at its website *sba.gov.* SBA experts suggest that you ask yourself these two questions:

1. How much can you realistically afford to invest and how much can you afford to lose?
2. And, have you ever owned or managed a business?

If you have no small business experience and you're risking money you cannot afford to lose, then buying a franchise or starting a business is a mistake.

If you do jump in, you may soon realize that you're paying all your bills…. employees, rent, loans, taxes and insurance…but you can't afford to pay yourself. That's where goals come in. How long can you give the business before you must make an income? Do you need a certain income?

"Get a written substantiation of any income projections, or income or profit claims from your franchiser," the SBA says. "This is required by the Federal Trade Commission (FTC) when a franchiser tells you can earn from investing in their franchise. If they do not have one or refuse to provide you with this information, they may have made a false claim."

Also think twice about buying into an existing franchise business in a corporation that has been recently purchased by a private equity group and no longer is operated by the original franchise founder. Equity groups are there to squeeze more profits out of the operation, not to take care of franchisees. Without mutual trust, the company may begin to rot from the inside. According to the SBA, a quality franchise provides help in several key areas including product development and services, store locations, market area guarantees and a quality corporate management team.

Franchise buying tips from *buyingafranchise.org*

- **Look at several franchise options** that fit your interests and your passions. Avoid in-home businesses.
- **Get advice.** Get independent advice from your banker, attorney and an accountant. Talk to franchise owners already in the business. Are franchisees getting the training

and support they need to be successful? Visit owners in different locations so they don't view you as competition.

- **Get the list of recent store closures.** Call a couple of ex-owners who closed or sold stores and find out why.

- **Decide if you have the skills to make the franchise a success.** Do you like accounting/bookkeeping? Will the franchise operator train you? The "fit" is critical.

- **Consider the franchiser's finances.** How long have they been in business? Do they have healthy accounts? Have they sued franchise operators? Carefully, read the franchise agreement.

- **Check out local market conditions.** What will the competition be like? What about a ready labor force? Do you get a restricted or exclusive franchise territory?

DISCLOSURE STATEMENT

Your franchiser should provide you with a franchise disclosure document. This is usually a 50-plus page book, says Jim Deitz at *franchisedoc.com* that gives you a clear idea of what the relationship will be like: Length of the agreement, territory, responsibilities, opportunities, costs. Read carefully through the financial history of the corporation.

Before you put your cash and your long-term future on the line take time to understand the risks and rewards of a franchise business.

FOR MORE:

"Consumer's Guide to Buying a Franchise," *Federal Trade Commission*

buyingafranchise.org/franchise-tips

"The Buyout of America," *by Josh Kosman.*

buyingafranchise.org.

franchisedoc.com

REVERSE MORTGAGES.
MORE BAD THAN GOOD.

"Neither a borrower nor a lender be."

--William Shakespeare (1564-1616)

C onsumer groups including the federal Consumer Financial Protection Bureau are warning seniors about reverse mortgages.

At first glance, a reverse mortgage may seem like a good idea especially for elderly single women who may be short on income and want to stay in their homes. But there's plenty to worry about when signing up for these loans.

A reverse mortgage is a loan that draws on the equity in your house. Obviously only people who have paid off their mortgages or who have more value in their home than what's left on an existing mortgage can consider a reverse mortgage.

The idea is to draw down that equity with cash withdrawals over time. When the equity is gone or the homeowner dies, the lender sells the home to repay the debt.

Of course, there likely will be upfront loan fees and other early rewards for the lender. Meanwhile, the mortgage pays out the equity in your home as cash; your debt level rises and net worth from the equity, decreases.

According Reuters news service, the most popular reverse mortgage loan is the Home Equity Conversion Mortgage (HECM), which is administered and regulated by the U.S. Department of

Housing and Urban Development and insured by the Federal Housing Administration.

Repayment typically is triggered when a homeowner dies or moves out permanently and is typically funded through sale of the home. If the balance on a HECM is higher than the value of the home, the FHA makes up the difference. (That's taxpayer money)

BORROWING TOO SOON

A growing number of borrowers are taking on reverse mortgage loans at younger ages in return for large lump payouts that carry high fixed rates of interest. Many of these loans are at risk of default, says the federal Consumer Financial Protection Bureau.

Borrowers may think that taking a fixed-rate loan is the best way to go. But according to the experts, fixed-rate lump sum loans rack up higher interest costs and deplete borrowers' equity far more rapidly.

While reverse mortgages may offer seniors in need a useful way to tap home equity, the CFPB found that **reverse loans are too complex for most seniors to understand**. Many homeowners struggle to understand the rising balance and falling equity structure of the loans, or do not understand that reverse mortgages really are loans.

WHO SHOULD CONSIDER A REVERSE MORTGAGE?

Only those over age 70 with plenty of equity value in their homes should consider a reverse mortgage. For women that age consideration should probably be much later, maybe age 80 since women typically outlive men.

LOOK AT AN ADJUSTABLE RATE LOAN

Indeed, if you decide to go with a reverse mortgage use an adjustable rate loan and only withdraw what you need over time, not in a lump sum. Taking a lump sum loan, leaves you with "no flexibility or cushion," say CFPB advisers.

Be sure you really understand what you're getting into especially if the loan agreement changes who has title to your home. Some deals mean the borrower ends up owing more than the value of the equity in their homes. When they die, the kids must come up with the difference.

When looking at a reverse mortgage get good outside financial advice. Talk to an elder law attorney, a financial adviser or an accountant. **Family members may NOT be the best source of advice since they may like the idea of tapping into your assets as an early inheritance, especially if they are hurting for money.**

The financial protection bureau warns that seniors are taking reverse mortgages too early, that they do not understand the agreements and are ending up defaulting on these loans.

They then lose their homes and have no money other than Social Security to live on into their real old age. **Final warning: A reverse mortgage is risky.**

FOR MORE:
  Federal Consumer Financial Protection Bureau at
    consumerfinance.gov
  Federal Trade Commission, "Reverse Mortgages" at ftc.gov
  "Reverse Mortgage Scams Proliferate," at reversemortgage.net

---

Julia Anderson

GET "SENIOR DEALS!"
BALANCE YOUR BUDGET

"*I learned a woman is <u>never</u> an old woman.*"

-- Joni Mitchell, American singer-songwriter, (1943 -)

A 60-something friend waited in line behind an older man at Wendy's. She heard him ask for his "senior discount." The woman at the register apologized and charged him less for his meal.

I asked the man what the discount was. He told me that seniors over age 55 get 10 percent off everything on the menu, every day. My friend said, "Being of that age myself, I figured I'd go for the discount too."

This prompted an Internet search that produced lists of restaurants, stores and supermarkets offering discounts to seniors using "discounts for seniors" in the search box on Google. There are plenty. Some offer email updates on new deals.

Checking into this stuff could become a full-time occupation but having a list handy can save money and time. These discounts are not automatic...you must ask!!

SAVING MONEY ON EVERYTHING

Emily Brandon, senior editor for retirement news at *usnews.com* has put together a "how to" book for seniors offering strategies that will save you money in retirement. The book is called *"Pensionless: The 10-step Solution to Stress-Free Retirement."*

She also writes a "planning to retire" blog. You can find it at *money.usnews.com.*

The Wall Street Journal recommends these money and retirement columnists and writers: Jonathan Clements, Jason Zweig, Kimberly Blanton and Christine Benz. Or try Jan Cullinane's book, *"The Single Women's Guide to Retirement."* All worth reading.

Financial writer **Brett Arends**, writing at MarketWatch, Fidelity and the Wall Street Journal offers these great ways to save money in retirement:

- **Use loyalty programs** to get discounts on car rental, air travel and other deals. Credit cards may offer huge bonuses like a free airline ticket to new customers.

- **Switch banks** and credit-card companies for less expensive services. Drop cards that charge fees.

- **Cut the frequency of services** such as pedicures and house cleaners. Leave the car in the garage, ride a bike.

- **Axe the landline** and switch to a new Internet and phone provider.

- **Refinance** the mortgage home.

- **Use warehouse clubs** by teaming with trusted friends or neighbors to make purchases.

- **Don't pay someone else to do what you can do yourself.** Your federal taxes, for instance. Home maintenance, for another.

- Use eBay and Craigslist. Buy for less.

- **Cut back on new books.** Download classics from *Gutenberg.org* for free or borrow on-line from your library.

- **Save on vacation deals.** Use last minute websites such as *vacationstogo.com* to find savings on vacation deals. Use *Airbnb.com* instead of paying for a hotel.

- **Go green.** Stop wasting hot water and cut your heating bill by purchasing new lower-flow aerator showerheads and using cold water to wash clothes. Slowly move to LED and CFL lighting in your home. Buy a "smart strip" to turn off peripheral electronics when not in use.

- **Volunteer** to get in to music events for free.

- **Go to happy hour** for lower prices on drinks and food plates. Get the early afternoon movie discount.

- **"Return sanity to the holidays,"** Arends advises. Set a budget, swap ornaments instead of spending big bucks on gifts people may not need or want.

Plenty of my women friends are finding great ways to cut costs and maintain budgets while living with style. One friend house-sits all over Southern California in some very nice homes.

FOR MORE:
frugalliving.com
giftcardgranny.com
seniordiscounts.com
vacationstogo.com

Julia Anderson

ANTIQUES AND COLLECTIBLES: NO ONE WANTS MY BROWN FURNITURE

"I also have intense relationships with furniture...probably because we practically had none when I was growing up."

--Barbara Streisand, actress, filmmaker. (1942 -)

PBS's Antiques Roadshow does what it calls 'vintage' episodes where appraisals made on the show 10 or 15 years ago are revalued in the current post-recessionary resale market. Often the values have declined. No surprise.

It turns out that our children and certainly our grandchildren are not interested in grandmother's mahogany bureau with the cute pull-down writing table, interior slots for envelopes and stationery and storage drawers.

For them, a piece of dark brown desk furniture makes no sense in a world of IKEA, laptops and Snapchat.

Unfortunately, that mahogany bureau has sentimental value for me. I picture my grandmother sitting next to it in her small living room while doing embroidery. My house is full of that kind of stuff – furniture, table clothes, cut crystal and grandmother's quilts and needle work.

The emotional baggage tied up with this could fill a barn. I wonder about what I'm going to do with it all. In conversations with friends, we ask the same questions. Then we laugh and shrug. What ARE we going to do with our stuff when we downsize?

FOLLOWING THE TRENDS

Every July, Portland, Ore. hosts one of the biggest antique and collectible show in the U.S. The event is held at the city's EXPO Center, and attracts 1,400 vendors and 16,000 visitors over two days. Everything is on display from antique woodworking tools to wind-up clocks, vintage jewelry to movie posters, and neon signs. Christine Palmer of Portland-based Palmer & Associates has been part of show for 30 years and now owns the show promotion and production business. Here's what she told me.

Collectibles and antiques evoke a childhood memory of something we experienced or something we wish we had owned. For me those memory-triggers include Western art, cowboy lamps, pictures of horses and for some reason that I don't understand, tin toy motorcycles and cobalt blue glassware. I've collected them for years.

But like everything else, the antique-collectible business is changing as the baby boomer generation approaches retirement. The last of us are in our 50s. With all the downsizing yet to come that prized family heirloom may have become (I hate to say it) junk.

WHAT'S NOT IN DEMAND

According to Palmer and others, glassware -- those crystal goblets your mother or grandmother so lovingly placed on their Thanksgiving dinner tables – is less collectible and less valuable. No one is buying formal glassware because no one is hosting a formal Thanksgiving or Christmas dinner. No one even wants the formal dining room table.

Upholstered sofas, china hutches, formal dining sets, wood-finished dressers, even pianos have become almost impossible to sell or even give away.

In the online Wall Street Journal, search for the article, *"Why the Market for Heirloom and Second-hand Furniture Has Disappeared."*

No one wants brown furniture reports Alina Dizik in the Wall Street Journal story. Antique oak tables and bedroom sets, Victorian-style mahogany – if it's brown, forget it.

ARE THERE ANY BUYERS?

Palmer said the antique business is alive, but the buyer profile is changing and what they want to buy is evolving. Buyers are 40-year-olds (and younger) who are furnishing their first or second home. They are looking for what the industry calls "mid-20th Century Casual." That includes 1950s dishes in bright colors, '50s and '60s table clothes and other textiles.

Younger buyers like decorative outdoor garden items -- the smallish wrought iron table with glass top and two matching chairs. Again, it's casual, not formal or fussy.

Vintage clothing is popular. By vintage, we're talking 1930s to the 1970s. The category includes hats, shoes, dresses, jackets and eyewear.

Vintage toys.... G.I. Joe and Star Wars action figures, lunch boxes from the 1980s -- are selling. A generation or two earlier, it was Gene Autry and the Lone Ranger.

Forty years ago, there was no IKEA or Target or imports from China. Families ate around a dining table separate from the kitchen. Now it's one big happy free-for-all bar-style meal.

THE AGE OF CONSUMPTION IS OVER

The demographic shift under way now has baby boomers downsizing after 50 years of post-World War II consumption at the same time as Millennials are becoming minimalists. The resale market is glutted with household stuff nobody wants.

Items in the general antique category have lost 50 percent or more of their value since the late 1990s, say some reports. Young families that once bought second-hand furniture or took hand-me-downs, now want new but cheap and sleek imports ala IKEA.

Palmer is confident that Portland's EXPO Center will continue to host big antique shows. The antique business, she said, is not dead but in flux. The Internet has certainly been a part of the change; it's easy to sell items like dolls, or wall paper or other small items online.

Did you know some people collect vintage swim suits and make them into wall displays? Vintage office supplies ala AMC's "Mad Men" drama series is a fresh collectible trend, says Country Living magazine.

WHAT TO EXPECT

Selling antiques and collectibles can be a fun part-time business in retirement but you've got to be prepared to sell online, to sell at shows and to maintain a niche sales display in an "antique mall." The three-way combination can pay off in revenue with little expense. That said, big old antique stores are gone, the "mall" with niche displays remain.

If you are ready to downsize:

- Find out what your kids want. Don't be hurt, if they're not interested in the "priceless" Spode china.
- Network with those in the business. What's selling, what's not? Ask about trends.
- Check out eBay, Craigslist and other online sales websites to determine values.
- Go to garage sales, estate sales and antique shows. Look at the prices.
- If you decide to have an estate sale, do your homework. (see tips below) Interview several estate sale business owners before choosing one.
- Get real about values of your priceless items. It won't hurt as much later when you try to sell or give them away. Your stuff, especially your brown furniture, may be worth a lot less than you think. Sorry.

DOWNSIZING?
HOW TO HIRE A REPUTABLE
ESTATE SALE BROKER

"Change before you have to."

-- Jack Welch, former General Electric Co. CEO. (1935 -)

When my mother, at age 95, moved into assisted living after hip surgery, she turned to me and said she was sorry for leaving behind her house full of stuff. It was pretty much jammed with collectibles, clothes, old and new, photos, dishware, kitchen things and a basement where she had "stored" left-overs from the estate sales of her mother and brother when they died. Hopefully it won't be that way for me (or for you).

If you don't want to handle downsizing on your own, you can use an estate sale service. Like all such businesses, some are good at what they do, and some are not. Some may be scammers. A woman I know recently contracted to have pieces of her mother's expensive furniture sold through an outside firm. More than a year later, she has yet to receive any money from the deal and now doubts that she ever will.

Scammers are a growing problem in the estate sale business where there is little regulation or recourse. Getting a signed contract in advance of the sale is a good first step. Make sure the commission is included in the contract. The best way to make sure the contract is followed is to attend the estate sale, even if your broker requests that you not be there.

Questions to ask before hiring an estate sale service:

- Can you provide references from the past six months?
- Are you bonded and insured?
- Will you provide a written statement of services?
- How are you paid: commission or flat fee?
- If commission, what percentage of sales will you charge?
- How long do you take to prepare and conduct the sale?
- Will you write receipts for all sold items?
- What other services do you offer: Boxing, bagging, clearing out leftovers, readying a home for sale?
- How soon after the sale will I be paid the money owed me?
- Do you prepare a written daily accounting and final accounting with receipts and inventory of items sold?

Source: *www.graceful-exits.com.*

A 'HOW-TO' ON ESTATE SALES

Patsy Rushing is never sure what she might find when she meets with a client who wants her services for an estate sale.

"It could be a family that's cleaning out the home of a favorite aunt who is downsizing to assisted living or a baby boomer couple going to a smaller home," said Rushing, who owns and operates an estate sale business in Vancouver, Washington.

Whatever the circumstances, Rushing advises those thinking of holding an estate sale to "not throw anything out." That's because what may be one person's junk is another's treasure. Old wall paper rolls, for instance. Or Christmas wrapping paper and magazines from the '40s.

"Just because something is old and dusty doesn't mean it might not have value," Rushing said. Her "don't toss" tip is one of many that professionals in the estate sale business offer to those who want to downsize.

GROWING DEMAND

Demand for estate sale services is growing as baby boomers age or must find help after the death of an elderly parent.

In the Portland, Ore. and Vancouver, Wash. market a website *estatesale-finder.com* lists more than 50 upcoming sales in the metro area scheduled over the next several months. Similar websites in other locations throughout the country do the same thing.

Karen Rhinehart, of Gaston, Ore., who operates a Portland area estate sale website, says that typically there are as many as 25 sales on any given weekend, year-round.

"People are kind of fanatic about estate sales and garage sales here," Rhinehart said. "There are lots of eBayers looking for resale items. Second-hand books are a strong seller because of our book stores and we're kind of an artsy town."

As many as 100 or 200 people might be lined up to get into a 'good' sale on the first morning, she said.

HOW ESTATE SALES WORK

Typically, estate sales are conducted over several days. It may take two weeks or longer to set up a sale with good displays, with items priced, labeled and advertised. Most estate sale services charge a commission ranging from 25 to 35 percent of gross sale revenue.

Estate agents should be willing to provide a written contract, references from recent sale clients and guarantee receipts for all items sold with a list. Some services will box or bag unsold items and take them to a donation center. Some will clean the house, readying it for sale or rent, all for additional fees. Most services will not take on a sale unless it will produce a minimum of $1,500 to $3,000.

Check into websites in your area that advertise upcoming estate sales. These sites can accommodate photos of your most sellable items. Newspaper advertising most often allows for both a print ad and an online posting on the paper's local website for double-coverage advertising.

Experts say that no matter what your route to downsizing, take time to research the value of what you are selling. Do a search at online sites for similar items for sale and check the price of recently sold items in the same category.

You can always go the garage sale route, but that means you do all the work yourself and you must haul off all the unsold items.

BASIC ESTATE SALE TIPS:

#1 - Trust the estate sale appraisal price.

#2 - Don't throw anything away. Old wallpaper is collectible.

#3 - Give the kids and your family their shot. Get family and the items they want out of the way before bringing in the estate sale service.

If you're cleaning out the house of a dotty old aunt, make sure you check all containers (even old pizza boxes) before discarding them. "One old lady was eating out of cottage cheese containers and begging her nieces for money," said Beverly Amundson, an estate sale broker. "Turns out she had $30,000 in savings bonds and cash hidden in sock drawers and a pizza box."

FOR MORE:
Estatesales-finder.com
Freefromclutter.com
Estatesales.org
Foursales.biz

TIMESHARE CONTRACTS:
GETTING IN
AND SAFELY GETTING OUT

*"Almost everything will work again if you
unplug it for a few minutes. Including you."*

-- Anne Lamott, novelist, essayist. (1954 -)

Nine million American households have purchased timeshare contracts, reports the American Resort Development Assn. With an estimated 1,500 timeshare resorts in the U.S. and some 121,000 vacation properties worldwide, there is a lot to choose from when searching for that piece of paradise.

The good news is that the industry has come a long way from the 1970s when timeshare properties were marketed with shady come-ons and high-pressure, misleading sales tactics. Consumer Reports magazine says, the "industry has become more consumer friendly and transparent" in the past 15 years.

BIG PLAYER TREND

That's because major hospitality companies -- Disney, Four Seasons, Hilton and Marriott – now are among the big timeshare players and have made the industry more attractive and reputable.

These days you can shop online, or chat live with a property representative to get detailed information about the costs of ownership, including the buy-in fee and ongoing annual maintenance costs.

For many, the timeshare concept makes sense: Multiple individuals share rights to use a property, each with his or her own allotted time frame --- usually a fixed week each year. Often now called, "vacation ownership" or "interval travel" programs, the idea is to get an affordable vacation at a luxury location.

In just 2014 alone, investors bought almost $8 billion worth of timeshare properties in the U.S. The average sale price was $20,020 with an average ongoing maintenance fee of $880 a year.

Median age of timeshare owners is 51. However, the median age of more recent buyers is 39, half have children younger than 18. Newer owners are younger, more affluent, more diverse and better educated.

The experts recommend that you consider this a lifestyle investment, not a financial investment. Don't expect to get your money back.

Get out your calculator and 'average out' your annual vacation expenses in prior years. If you're paying $100 a night in annual timeshare maintenance fees for a week's stay and you already paid $20,000 for that week's stay upfront, it doesn't make sense to pay full retail price for a timeshare.

The reality is that there are many timeshare properties for sale at a fraction of their original cost. The Internet offers tips for how to get a good deal by buying a resale rather than paying full-price from a developer/owner.

TIMESHARE BUYING TIPS

Before you jump into a timeshare investment, ask yourself these questions:

1. Are you committed to vacationing every year?
2. Will the resort you are considering stand the test of time?
3. How much will you be spending on vacations in the next 10 years?

When buying new or a resale make sure the written contract contains all the promises made during the pitch. You could run the contract by a timeshare attorney. Know what the cancellation policy is in case you change your mind. Talk to other owners in the timeshare you are considering. What is their level of satisfaction with the property?

Experts say buy-in with a flat upfront fee. Don't buy over time. And be prepared to manage your contract going forward, which may be complicated. The program might include a "point system," for usage and upgrades. There may be changes in ownership and tiered memberships.

SELLING A TIMESHARE: WATCH OUT FOR SCAMS!

Selling a timeshare property contract is where the industry still wallows in potential scams. A resale service may offer to unload your timeshare for an upfront fee.

Then the resale service may ask for more money for marketing. You finally realize that they are NOT selling your timeshare, but just taking your money. Lots of consumer complaints about this.

Recently, a timeshare resale operator was charged with fraud by the Feds for bilking timeshare property owners out of $15 million by charging up-front fees based on false promises. **Legitimate fees are typically paid after a sale is concluded.**

As for resale value, a timeshare is more like a car than a house because timeshare properties depreciate. There is no shortage of websites including eBay, RedWeek, and Timeshare Resale Vacations that advertise timeshares for $1. That's because the owner/seller wants out, <u>badly</u>.

FOR MORE:
   Federal Trade Commission Website at *consumer.ftc.gov*
   American Resort Development Association at *arda.org.*

Julia Anderson

Estate Planning: Now, Not Later

Dying doesn't worry me. What happens to my money and furniture when I'm gone doesn't worry me. However, I do worry about what happens when (and if) I become too old to manage my own affairs.

As she aged into her 90s, my mother became truly disabled because of poor eyesight, ill health and slipping mental acuity. She needed help paying her power bill, her taxes and managing her finances.

My mother turned to a bank trust department for assistance. That was at age 95 when she moved from her home to assisted living. Years earlier, she had legally set up the bank trust. It was just a matter of letting go of the reins.

Planning the last phase of your life is about trust and about timing. People slip into senility without noticing. They don't want trouble with their kids. Making changes becomes more difficult. I wonder if I will know when it's time? I worry about who gets the reins.

Julia Anderson

ESTATE PLANNING BASICS: AVOIDING MISTAKES

"The whole plot (of Downton Abbey) is really an enormous estate-planning problem."

--Kenneth Brier, Wall Street Journal

1. **Make a will.** In a will, you state who you want to inherit your assets.

2. **Consider a trust.** By holding your property in a living trust, your survivors won't have to go through probate court, a time-consuming and expensive process.

3. **Health care directives.** Write out your wishes for health care.

4. **Assign Power of Attorney.** With a durable power of attorney for finances, you can give a trusted person authority to handle your finances and property if you become incapacitated and unable to handle your own affairs.

5. **Beneficiary forms.** Name beneficiaries for bank accounts and retirement plans makes the account automatically "payable on death" to your beneficiary.

6. **Funeral expenses.** Set up a payable-on-death expense account at your bank and deposit funds into it to pay for your memorial/funeral and related expenses.

7. **Final arrangements.** Make your wishes known regarding organ and body donation and disposition of your body (burial or cremation). Give instructions to your heirs, now.

8. **Documents.** Make sure your attorney-in-fact and/or your executor has access to your important documents.

Those who followed Downton Abby, the television saga of a few years ago, learned a lot about what not to do when it comes to estate planning.

As the upper-class Crawley family emerged from the Victorian era, struggled through World War I, and made it to the modern age, mistakes popped up at every turn. Better estate planning would have eliminated the trauma and the drama.

Estate planning is not just for the rich. Anyone who owns a home or other real estate, anyone who owns a family business or has investments can learn from the Downton story that hinges on a series of financial set-backs, surprises and losses.

Here's what we learned:

SELL THE HOUSE.

Inheriting an old house is more trouble than it's worth. The Crawley family is saddled with a huge old house and sprawling estate that requires nearly all their money and a huge staff to maintain. Parents may over-estimate the sentimental attachment of their children to the old family home. It is hard for a family to agree on how to manage an old property, especially if one of them wants to live in it.

SPELL OUT CONTROL AND OWNERSHIP WHEN PASSING ON A FAMILY-OWNED BUSINESS.

Sons-in-Law (as in the Crawley family) may have different ideas about how a family business should be run. Make sure everybody is clear on who has voting rights, veto rights and the power to fire. Expect tension as the transition is made from parents to the new generation.

USE (LEGAL) TRUSTS TO PROTECT ASSETS.

Trusts can be helpful to two reasons -- tax planning and money management. A corporate trustee is a professional who is bound by investing rules. A trustee knows investments must be diversified and that actions must be reported back to the trustee and the trustee's family, in some cases monthly.

While your nephew Tony is a nice guy, he may not understand finances or investing. Furthermore, he has no legal responsibility to tell anyone what he's doing with your money or property. Go the bank trust route.

MAKE A WILL.

Have a will and business agreement in place for what would happen to your spouse and children if you die. Update this will every few years.

SET UP MEDICAL DIRECTIVES.

Sybil, the youngest Crawley daughter dies giving birth. The family struggles to guess what her wishes would have been regarding her medical care or what religious faith she wished her baby to be baptized in. A will and a medical directive would have been useful.

DIVERSIFY YOUR ASSETS.

Things get sticky for the Crawley family when the Earl of Grantham loses his fortune – all his wife Cora's money --- by investing in a Canadian railway company that goes bankrupt. It's never a good idea to put all your money into one investment. Are you unsure of your investment strategy? *Investor.gov* is a good place to start learning more. Thank you, Downton Abbey for these family money management lessons as true today as 100 years ago.

FOR MORE:
investor.gov
investor.gov
wise-investors.org
wiseswomeninvestor.org
learnvest.com
bankrate.com

Julia Anderson

WRITE A WILL:
DO EVERYONE A FAVOR

"There's no love without tears;
there's no happiness without sacrifice;
and there's no forever without goodbye."

--Unknown

There are many reasons to have a will but among the most important may be to keep your heirs from fighting over who is in charge and who gets your money when you die.

DON'T WORRY ABOUT PLAYING FAVORITES.

It is best if **one person** (family member or outside trusted adviser) takes on the job of executor in settling your estate.

With second and third marriages, assigning an executor to administer the settlement of an estate could be essential to preserving harmony among children, step-children and grandchildren. Even in a first marriage there may be tension among family members.

"The fact is everyone should have a will," says Karey Schoenfeld, former president of the Oregon Society of Certified Public Accountants and a Vancouver, Wash. attorney who specializes in estate planning. "A will puts someone in charge."

The sad news is that only 55 percent of adult Americans have gone to the trouble of writing a will. That leaves their heirs to pick up the pieces after they die.

WHY HAVE A WILL?

- To make sure that when you die, your assets are distributed as you want.
- To name an executor who will distribute your estate at your death.
- To appoint a trustee for adult children who may need help with finances.
- To save on estate taxes and inheritance taxes.
- To leave some or all your assets to charity.

PUTTING A WILL IN PLACE

You can write a will yourself using a standard form printed off the Internet. Ideally, the forms are state-specific, since laws regulating estate settlement vary from state to state. *Forbes.com* offers pros and cons on the low-cost do-it-yourself strategy. Get this document notarized at a bank or law office.

Or use an attorney to tailor a will to your specific wishes and needs. Much depends on your family dynamics, what you can afford and the size of your estate.

For those with estates of $1 million and more, a will may be essential for tax-planning purposes or trust designation. But even people with modest estates may want to give money or property to a favorite charity or to a favorite grandchild who might otherwise be ignored.

If you have these needs or have a family that might disagree, you likely need a will that deals with more than what an online form can cover, Schoenfeld said.

BASIC LEGAL DOCUMENTS

A will is one of three basic legal documents (usually written as a package) that women (and all seniors) should have in place.

Others are:

- A **durable power of attorney** that designates someone who can step in to run your affairs when you can no longer take care of things such as day-to-day bill-paying, investing or managing other aspects of your estate.

- A **power of attorney for health care decisions** that designates someone to step in if you fall ill or are a victim of dementia and cannot make health care decisions for yourself.

These legal directives, along with a will, should be reviewed at least every five years to make sure they remain valid. Make sure these legal documents are state-specific.

AVOIDING HEART ACHE

A will should state who handles your affairs and who should receive your personal property - paintings, jewelry and furniture - when you die. It may cover how grandchildren might receive certain assets and in what form.

"Occasionally, a client will say they don't care what happens to their estate after they die," Heidi Johnson Bixby, a certified financial planner in Vancouver, Wash. told me. "Maybe it's because they don't want to confront their death. I tell them that even if they don't care what happens, a will can simplify things for their heirs in a time of grieving. A will is about leaving a legacy," Bixby said. "Part of that legacy could be about the mess and the hassle you leave behind if you don't write a will."

A will should also consider the financial situation of family members. For instance, without a will, any children receiving disability payments could see their benefits ruined by unexpected inheritance. Or a child with IRS tax trouble could affect how the estate is settled.

COST IS A FACTOR

Using an attorney to write your will typically costs several hundred dollars or more. My last will cost $2,000 and that was at a discount. Filling out a state-specific form off a website and getting it notarized is much less expensive, but make sure it does what is needed.

SEPARATE LOCATION FOR FUNERAL INSTRUCTIONS

Funeral instructions and burial instructions should be written up separately and given to family members. Heirs typically don't get around to looking at a will until after the funeral. Your funeral and burial instructions may be overlooked if they are kept with your will.

MORE REASONS FOR A WILL

If you want to leave any part of your assets to charity, you need a will. If you want to benefit both family members and a charity, a will is essential. There may be ways to reduce taxes for your family through special charitable trust arrangements. An attorney with expertise in these areas will be helpful.

FOR MORE:

American Bar Association, *Americanbar.org*

How to Write a Will, *USA.gov*

NOLO.com

Seniorlaw.com

FINANCIAL ABUSE – PART ONE: WOMEN ARE MORE VULNERABLE

"You shall not steal, nor deal falsely,
nor lie to one another."

--Leviticus 19:11

It may begin innocently enough with a family member dropping in to help an elderly parent pay monthly bills. It may be a live-in caregiver who begins calling his client "mom."

Or the friendly financial adviser who offers to manage a large investment portfolio for an elderly couple whom he has met at church.

At some point the person paying the monthly bills is spending the elderly person's money and giving themselves an early inheritance. The caregiver has his elderly patron rewrite her will giving him half million dollars when she dies.

The financial manager cannot resist the temptation to tap into his clients' nest egg, stealing more than $1 million.

These scenarios all are true examples of a growing national problem -- financial exploitation of the elderly. Nine times out of 10 the abuse is by a family member and experts estimate that only one in 25 cases ever is reported.

Older people are living longer. Older people have all the money. That imbalance can tear families apart as siblings compete for parental favor and money and giving unscrupulous caregivers opportunities to steal.

In some cases, what may have started out as a workable plan to help mom turns into a nightmare with the elderly parent trapped in their own home in an abusive and controlling relationship, experts say. Women generally are at higher risk because they tend to out-live their spouses.

"Thieves...family members or not...count on their abusive behavior to not come to light," Dianna Kretzschmar, program coordinator for a new Elder Abuse Justice Center in Vancouver, Washington, told me.

The center is the first like it in Washington state where the latest statewide data show more than 42,000 abuse cases were reported in 2016, up from 14,400 cases in 2008.

Twenty-five percent of the cases involved some type of financial exploitation.

Kretzschmar sees the center's case load expanding "exponentially" compounded by a growing generational gap between haves and have nots.

"Our elderly are generally those who came out of the Depression, who saved and didn't have credit cards," she said. "They didn't take on debt and they lived within their means. They are not equipped to handle the world we have now...frankly they're sitting ducks."

WEALTH GAP

The wealth gap between younger and older Americans is the greatest that it has ever been. Households headed by people 65 and older have a net worth 47 times greater than households headed by someone under 35. That's the greatest spread ever and five times worse than it was just a few years ago before the Great Recession.

With the baby boomer population wave heading into retirement the number of seniors 65 and older in the U.S. population is expected to increase from 39.6 million in 2009 to 72.1 million in 2030.

Experts at the National Center on Elder Abuse say that as elders become more physically frail, they're less able to stand up to bullying or to fight back if attacked. They may not see or hear as well or think as clearly as they used to, leaving openings for unscrupulous people to take advantage of them."

On the other hand, mental or physical ailments may make them more difficult companions for the people who live with them, thus creating an atmosphere of entitlement.

More than half a million reports of abuse against elderly Americans reach authorities every year, and millions more cases go unreported.

ABUSE TAKES MANY FORMS

- Physical abuse. Physical elder abuse is non-accidental use of force against an elderly person that results in physical pain, injury, or impairment. Such abuse includes not only physical assaults but inappropriate use of drugs, restraints, or confinement.

- Emotional abuse. In emotional or psychological senior abuse, people speak to or treat elderly persons in ways that cause emotional pain or distress.

- Financial abuse. That may mean slowly taking over the elderly person's check book and using it to pay for unrelated personal expenses. It may mean using the elderly homeowner's money to buy unwanted items such as TVs, appliances and cars. Or it could mean "borrowing" from a savings account and never paying it back, talking the person into an unneeded reverse mortgage or repeatedly pushing a vulnerable person into bad investments with high commissions.

SPOTTING ELDER ABUSE

The National Center on Elder Abuse offers these tips for spotting abuse:

- Intimidation through yelling or threats. Behavior from the elder that mimics dementia, such as rocking, sucking, or mumbling to oneself. Humiliation and ridicule.

- Non-verbal psychological elder abuse can take the form of ignoring the elderly person, isolating an elder from friends or activities and terrorizing or menacing the elderly person.

- Financial abuse may mean big withdrawals from the elder's accounts or sudden changes in the elder's financial condition. Items or cash may be missing from the senior's household. Suspicious changes in wills, power of attorney, titles, and policies are a clue. Addition of names to the senior's bank signature card.

- Other signs: Unpaid bills or lack of medical care, although the elder has enough money to pay for them. Financial activity the senior couldn't have done, such as an ATM withdrawal when the account holder is bedridden. Unnecessary services, goods, or subscriptions. In addition, health care fraud may victimize an elder by using duplicate billings to "gain" the system, overmedication to obtain drugs and inadequate care even though bills are paid.

REPORTING ABUSE CAN BE ANONYMOUS

"All you're saying is that you think there might be something wrong, that you have concerns. APS investigates and may find nothing, or findings may be inconclusive. We need to remember that the triumph of evil is for good people to do nothing," she said.

REPORTING ELDER ABUSE

If you suspect elder abuse, call Adult Protection Services in your area where staff is available to investigate possible cases.

To anonymously report elder abuse: Call National Center on Elder Abuse, Elder care Hot Line: 800-677-1116

Nationwide Hot Line: 855-500-3537

National Center for Elder Abuse website: *ncea.aoa.gov.*

Oregon state: 866-406-4287.

Washington state: 866-363-4276.

Julia Anderson

FINANCIAL ABUSE - PART TWO:
AVOIDING ELDER ABUSE

*"You'd be surprised what people will do for money
that they wouldn't do for love."*

-- Rachel Caine, author, (1962 -)

E lderly women are more frequently the victims of financial abuse simply because they often outlive their spouses. An aging population, a shifting economy and lack of wage growth are factors in the alarming increase in financial abuse cases. So is illegal drug use.

Nationally, an estimated one in 10 Americans aged 60 and older have experienced some form of elder abuse, reports the National Center on Elder Abuse.

Cases involve stealing money from checking accounts, stealing money from investment funds, refinancing an elderly person's home and taking the equity money.

Signing someone up for a reverse mortgage and taking the money, setting up unauthorized use of debit or credit cards.

The victim may never see the bank statement or the credit card bill and has no clue that anything is going on. Family members and caregivers can be tempted.

For instance, Eva, age 84, paid $500 for each trip a caregiver drove her 19 miles to town for grocery shopping.

In Oregon, females were the victims of financial abuse in 62 percent of the cases investigated and daughters (or daughters-in-law) were the most likely suspects.

Enforcement agencies say the cases are hard to prove because it's usually a family member who's doing the stealing and the elderly person is either clueless to the crime or reluctant to pursue a case against a child.

PREVENTION AND TRAINING

States are stepping up training for enforcement officials and are putting more information out to the public on how to report abuse. Banking associations are providing staff training to spot financial abuse. The Oregon Bankers Association distributes a prevention kit to bank employees and sells it to banks in other states.

Abuse cases can be reported anonymously. By calling a national number, you can connect with Adult Protection people in your community. That number is 855-500-3537 or go to the National Center for Elder Abuse at *ncea.aoa.gov.*

Many states have made it mandatory for clergy, nurses, senior center employees and physicians to report elder abuse. In Oregon the list now includes attorneys and other professionals.

WHAT TO DO

At some point, you likely will need help paying bills, managing your investments and your real estate. Hire a bank trust department to do it. *Bankrate.com* offers this basic trust information.

For a fee of 1 to 2 percent of total assets, a bank will pay all your bills, manage your assets and report back to you as required by law every month. The bank will provide for your derelict children who may be asking for financial help. A bank will make your best interests its top priority. It can be the financial gatekeeper. Typical fee for an attorney to draw up a trust is about $1,000 to $1,500. That's a real savings in the face of abuse by heirs or caregivers.

SENIOR HOUSING & LONG-TERM CARE. HOW MUCH WILL IT COST?

"Aging is not lost youth,
but a new stage of opportunity and strength."

-- Betty Friedan, American writer, feminist, activist. (1921-2006)

SENIOR HOUSING DEFINITIONS:

Independent Living: Communities for independent seniors that offer the conveniences of on-site recreation plus educational and social opportunities.

Assisted Living: Residential housing, assistance in daily activities, and some healthcare.

Continuing Care: Provide a continuum of care in one location from private units to assisted living and skilled nursing care

Skilled nursing care: Care in a hospital-like setting with nursing, physical therapy.

Alzheimer's Care or Memory Care: Promotes residents' individual skills and interests in an environment that helps to diminish confusion and agitation in a secure environment.

Adult day Care: Day-time care including meals in an organized setting with activities and services meant to promote well-being.

Adult family homes: Licensed residential homes with up to six residents. Services include room, board, laundry and necessary supervision along with help with daily living.

As we age, most of us expect to remain in our homes and hope to be there until the end. The reality is that according to national surveys, 70 percent of us over age 65 will likely need long-term care and/or will die in a hospital.

At the start, home care services may include drop-in help for bathing and meal preparation. As aging progresses, many of us will move to senior housing – independent living, assisted living, memory care or an adult family home.

Unless you are very low-income, you and/or your family will be paying for all or some of those services. Those costs can range up to more than $90,000 a year (2018) for skilled nursing services in a hospital-like setting after a stroke or other debilitating health problem.

Meanwhile, many of us in our 60s are looking for senior housing for our elderly mothers. Finding senior services for a loved one and investigating housing options and costs can feel overwhelming for families.

The good news is that help is available and it's free. State agencies throughout the nation offer help to families seeking help in finding senior housing and care.

But there are challenges in finding the right care at the right cost. Demand for senior housing in certain categories is outstripping supply. That means monthly rents and rates are increasing. Low-income senior housing is particularly in short supply.

The reality is that the more income you have the better your chances are of finding senior housing. But with the help of community services specialists, families can get started on tailoring local support resources with the individual senior's needs. These specialists know what questions families need to ask and what local services are available.

SENIOR HOUSING OUTLOOK

Demand for senior housing is growing as baby boomers age into their 70s and 80s. So, planning makes sense. Tips for helping an aging parent:

- Take stock of the personal situation of your senior.
- Assess the needed level of care.
- Look at the current financial picture and what might change.
- Work with a senior living advisor in your area to find solutions to the challenges your family might face.

Those advisors also are available through private services such as A Place for Mom, Assisted Living Locators, Adult Living Solutions.

Along with costs and services, family may also be considering location of the care facility. Location to and from work is very important for a family member who is employed and wants to check in with a loved one to or from work.

In their book, **"What You Really Need to Know for the Second Half of Your Life,"** the staff at law firm, Phelan Webber & Associates in Vancouver, Wash., points out that a socially active life style is beneficial at all stages of aging. Depending on the personality and care needs of a loved one, families may be able to arrange in-home companionship through Meals on Wheels, drop-in care services and family visits.

When the time comes, even though an elderly person may resist a move to a care facility, a good transition to a group home or assisted living facility may lower stress levels for everyone and provided that needed socialization for the senior, the Phelan experts say.

When a move is necessary, an assessment by a nurse is required to determine the patient's level of care needs. That level of care then dictates the level of services in a care facility. That translates into how much it will cost.

FOR MORE:

Eldercare locator, USA.gov

AARP Caregiving Resources, aarp.org

Senior Housing, HUD.gov

Medicare.gov/coverage/long-term-care.html

MONEY AND MENTAL ILLNESS: MANAGING FAMILY CHALLENGES

"When you are mad, mad like this,
you don't know it. Reality is what you see.
When what you see shifts, departing from anyone
else's reality, it's still reality to you."

-- Marya Hornbacher, author *"Madness: A Bipolar Life"*

There's no greater emotional or financial challenge facing women than dealing with a family member who is mentally ill whether it be a spouse, child or sister.

For me it was all three.

Some people who struggle with mental illness or a personality disorder can separate themselves from what's happening to their brains. They can recognize the problems, seek professional help and receive medications to bring their lives into normal ranges. Others can't. Their reality is what it is...theirs.

As my bi-polar sister angrily once told me, "Even if I end up living under a bridge with a grocery cart, don't worry about me." She was saying, back off. I can handle this.

For better or worse, she is. We don't talk much.

Family members with mental illness often become estranged from their parents or siblings because they see attempts to help as interference, as threatening and controlling.

When I married my first husband I did not see the mental challenges facing him – his outbursts of frustration and anger, his paranoid controlling attitude toward authority, his compulsive focus on detail that made very task, every outing, every conversation an endless stream-of-consciousness ordeal.

Neither did I recognize the problems my sister faced because of her manic-depressive condition – her inability to hold a job, her battles with authority and her life teetering on the edge of financial disaster. Both my ex-husband and my sister take medication to manage their brain chemistry and bring relative calm to their lives.

Both sides of this genetic pool came together in my older son who had a 'reality break' at age 21 during his sophomore year in college. He takes lithium, the standard treatment for bi-polar people. But his medical care has been inconsistent, plagued with shifting insurance coverage and multiple providers. Holding a demanding job has been difficult. Paying his bills and keeping up with his child support payments have been difficult.

A WAY FORWARD

In finding a way forward, I have my mother's experience with my sister to draw on.

According to **Money and Mental Health Policy Institute**, people with mental health problems are three times as likely to have problem debt.

Awhile back, I heard the compelling first-person story of a woman whose husband was bi-polar. His manic behavior over several years ended with his suicide. His behavior wrecked her life emotionally and financially for a long time.

Hearing her story, she was still wondering if she could have done something different to protect herself and her daughter from his destructive behavior and the financial train-wreck after his death.

But when you're in the middle of a relationship with someone you love who is ransacking family finances by not following through on business agreements and lying about it all, what action do you take?

Looking back, this woman adamantly recommended leaving the relationship if the person that you care about is not being honest with themselves and others. Get out of the relationship, if the person is secretive about money matters and defensive if you question their actions. For a parent it may not be that clear cut.

Over her life time, my mother gave my sister love and money in the hope that things would get better and that she would find her way. But as my mother aged into her 80s, my sister's financial requests became more persistent, more frequent.

When my mother agreed to write a $10,000 check to finance an ill-conceived lawsuit brought by my sister against a former employer, things were getting out of hand.

MORE OPEN DIALOGUE

Medical science has made mental illness in all its forms more diagnosable and more treatable. Society has become more open about mental illness. Progress with medications has helped people function in the real world.

There are organizations ready to provide support such as **NAMI, the National Alliance on Mental Illness** with its local chapters.

For parents, the core challenge remains. People with mental illness have a harder time holding a job because their brains sometimes whirl too fast or their obsessive focus on detail may become an enemy. Money, or lack of it, is a constant issue.

I know parents who have stuck by their schizophrenic children even as those children have ended up in trouble with the police. They have stuck with them to find housing, find a support group and get them in a safe place. Even after all that effort, things can fall apart. They start again.

Parents with bi-polar children may find themselves handing out money in an endless co-dependent relationship. That's OK, if you can do it without damaging your own finances and without short-changing your retirement.

Bottom Line: "The ill family member (or spouse) must recognize and accept the illness, be willing to receive treatment, and if possible, learn to manage the illness," experts at *HealthyPlace.com*, a mental health support website, say. "If the mentally ill spouse or child is not willing to do these things, it may become impossible for the family to continue to support him or her. The family is not required to throw away their own lives for someone who refuses to cooperate. There are limits."

My mother hated confrontation and never set real limits. But in her last years, shifting her own assets into a bank-managed trust account took the pressure off. She was no longer writing the checks. My sister had to ask the bank for money, rather than my mother.

It helped make her final years much more pleasant.

FOR MORE:
National Alliance on Mental Illness, NAMI.org
Money and Mental Health Policy Center,
 moneyandmentalhealth.org
MarriedtoMania.com (also a book by Elizabeth Atlas).
Healthline.com
Healthyplace.com
"Stop Walking on Eggshells: Taking Your Life Back When
 Someone You Care About Has Borderline Personality
 Disorder" by Paul Mason

BANK TRUSTS:
WILL YOUR TRUSTEE BE
A BANKER OR UNCLE LOUIE?

"Nearly every small town in America has a bank trust department, yet there seems to be this idea that trust funds are only for the super-rich."

-- TheBalance.com

WHAT'S A TRUST?

In law, a trust is a relationship where property is held by one party for the benefit of another party. A trust is created by the owner, called grantor, who transfers property to a trustee. The trustee holds that property for the trust's beneficiaries. The trustee then can control the property and its benefits if the grantor is absent, incapacitated, or dead. Trusts are frequently created in wills, defining how money and property will be handled for children or other beneficiaries.

Most people don't need trust management of their assets in their old age, but some do. Trusts are useful when there are substantial assets typically worth a combined $500,000 and up to be managed. But can be worth much less, if circumstances require outside help.

Trusts are useful if:

- If there are second, third and even fourth marriage situations with children and step-children. If the kids hate each other.
- If one of the kids is physically or morally incapable or is disabled.
- If there are a lot of assets and no ability to management them, yourself.

For the peace-of-mind it brought my family, I'd say bank trust management fees of 1.5 percent of assets to oversee my mom's investments, her checking and savings accounts, to pay most bills and operate the farm were worth it.

With limited eye-sight resulting from a stroke and general incapacity from old age, my mother at 95 was quickly losing control. She could not remember key conversations, was indecisive to the point of distraction and as her own attorney said, "played my sister and me off against each other when it came to money matters."

Was I totally comfortable with everything the bank trust department did or didn't do? No, but things settled down, my mother was less worried about her assets. The bank took care of my mother's needs while providing ongoing support for my bi-polar sister who continued to live in my mom's house on the farm.

Money issues no longer came up. My sister went to the bank with her funding requests.

My mother lived out her last three years in an assisted-living center in relative peace. The bank sent monthly updates on its management activities to my mother, to me and to my sister. Everyone calmed down.

ADVICE TO FAMILIES

Families that are considering setting up a legal trust must understand that every trust is unique in terms of individuals and assets, so it is important to tailor a trust document to those specifics. Pulling a formulaic document off the internet may not work, said my mom's bank trust manager.

"Do you pull your own teeth?" he asked. "It doesn't make sense to go to the internet to find some wacky form to dispose of everything you've worked your lifetime for, just to save money on attorney's fees."

Some families don't need a trust but instead just need a good up-to-date will and a durable power of attorney, he said. Families wishing to setup a trust should work with a knowledgeable attorney who draws up the documents.

REVIEW THE DOCUMENTS

Before signing those documents, they should be reviewed with the proposed trustee so that the family, the attorney and trustee (in this case the bank) agree on what is intended.

Secondly, people need to be careful about who they name as trustee.

My banker friend says, "If you decide that Uncle Louie should be the trustee, be sure you know what you and Uncle Louie are getting into. The best agreement isn't worth very much if you don't have a competent trustee, someone who will put in the time and provide regular reports on how things are going."

It may be flattering to be asked to be a trustee, but it's a big job for a family member, he said.

ACCOUNTABILITY OF TRUST MANAGERS

Bank trust departments and other financial institutions are legally bound to provide competent trust management. Policies and procedures are in place, reports must be prepared. Trust departments are audited by outside regulators. Uncle Louie, meanwhile, is not required to do anything.

"If the bank trustee is a jerk, you can call his boss," our banker said. "Professionally managed trusts are held to a higher standard than an individual. There's definitely recourse."

Professional trust managers have a duty to communicate, to keep an accounting, not to self-deal and to be impartial.

"Barring fraud or embezzlement, courts hold individuals as trustees to a much lower standard," he said. That is not to say that professional trust managers don't make mistakes. That's why they are insured, bonded, audited and reviewed.

LEGAL TERMINOLOGY

There's a lot of terminology around trusts. We started out proposing a conservatorship for my mother, but because she and my father, who had died 25 years earlier, already set up a couple of trusts, one in my dad's name and another in hers, a conservatorship wouldn't work.

The new trust provided oversight to the prior trusts. Our banker agreed that legal trust documents can be 'incomprehensible' to the non-professional. So even if you assign yourself as trustee of your own trust, it's a good idea to ask a bank or your CPA to provide what's called a document review. Ask the simple question: "How does this look to you?" Their suggestions likely will be worth it.

BANK MANAGEMENT FEES

Typically, trust management fees range from 1 to 2 percent of assets under management. The greater the trust assets, the lower the set fee. The grantor and beneficiaries are entitled to at least an annual accounting of the trust, most often quarterly or monthly.

The bank can be an agent or co-trustee. It can also be a successor trustee or an alternative trustee. As part of the estate planning process grantors should make a list of tangible assets and carefully spell out who gets what in terms of art work, furniture, cars, clothes and jewelry.

Our banker has seen 'train wrecks' where the kids are fighting, one party has carted off stuff and everyone is upset. Planning vastly increases your odds of success. "Having assets should be a blessing, not a curse," he said.

A CAUTION: Don't count on trust departments to do any heavy lifting when it comes to dysfunctional family members or confrontation. Trust department officers are NOT the police and are not keen on dealing with squatters or desk-pounding heirs.

A PLUS: When my mother died at almost age 99, the bank trust handled the disposition of her estate...the farm, the investments, everything. My sister and I just had to wait for all the paperwork to be filed and the distribution to be made.

FOR MORE:
"8 Ways to Avoid Probate," by Mary Randolph at nolo.com
Trust administration and wealth management, usbank.com

10 TIPS FOR HIRING A TAX PROFESSIONAL

"The hardest thing in the world to understand is taxes."

-- Albert Einstein (1879-1955)

Programming a new smart phone is nothing but a pain for me. I'd rather find a Verizon technician to help me muddle through the app downloads and email set-ups. But when it comes to doing my federal tax return, Bring it on!

Tax filing has been rewarding for two reasons: I save several hundred dollars by not having to pay a tax accountant, and I like the challenge of doing taxes myself, using the long-form and itemizing deductions.

All of that is changing, however, with the tax reform law passed by Congress in late 2017. With a substantial increase in the standard deduction, it may not make sense to itemize. Even so, you may want a tax professional to handle your tax return.

Here are 10 Tips for Hiring Tax Return Preparer:

1. **Check the preparer's qualifications.** New regulations require all paid tax return preparers to have a Preparer Tax Identification Number. In addition to making sure they have a PTIN, ask if the preparer is affiliated with a professional organization and attends continuing education classes. The IRS is also phasing in a new test requirement to make sure those who are not an enrolled agent, CPA, or attorney have met minimal competency requirements. Those subject to the test will become a Registered Tax Return Preparer once they pass it.

2. **Check on the preparer's history.** Check to see if the preparer has a questionable history with the Better Business

Bureau and check for any disciplinary actions and licensure status through the state boards of accountancy for certified public accountants; the state bar associations for attorneys; and the IRS Office of Enrollment for enrolled agents.

3. **Ask about their fees upfront.** Avoid preparers who base their fee on a percentage of your refund or those who claim they can obtain larger refunds than other preparers. Always make sure any refund due is sent to you or deposited into an account in your name. Under no circumstances should all or part of your refund be directly deposited into a preparer's bank account.

4. **Ask if they offer electronic filing.** Any paid preparer who prepares and files more than 10 returns for clients must file the returns electronically, unless the client opts to file a paper return. More than 1 billion individual tax returns have been safely and securely processed since the debut of electronic filing in 1990. Make sure your preparer offers IRS e-file.

5. **Make sure the tax preparer is accessible**. Make sure you will be able to contact the tax preparer after the return has been filed, even after the April due date, in case questions arise.

6. **Provide all records and receipts needed to prepare your return.** Reputable preparers will request to see your records and receipts and will ask you multiple questions to determine your total income and your qualifications for expenses, deductions and other items. Do not use a preparer who is willing to electronically file your return before you receive your Form W-2 using your last pay stub. This is against IRS e-file rules.

7. **Never sign a blank return.** Avoid tax preparers that ask you to sign a blank tax form. Such a move spells real trouble and potential for fraud.

8. **Review the entire return before signing it.** This seems like a given, but don't sign your tax return until you've reviewed it and asked questions. Make sure you understand everything and are comfortable with the accuracy of the

return before you sign it. You are legally responsible for what it says!!!

9. **Make sure the preparer signs the form and includes their PTIN.** A paid preparer must sign the return and include their PTIN as required by law. Although the preparer signs the return, you are responsible for the accuracy of every item on your return. The preparer must also give you a copy of the return.

10. **Report abusive tax preparers to the IRS.** You can report abusive tax preparers and suspected tax fraud to the IRS on Form 14157, Complaint: Tax Return Preparer. you can download Form 14157 from www.irs.gov or order by mail at by calling 800- 829-3676.

According to the IRS, something like 11 percent of returns sent in by professional tax preparers have problems and questionable calculations. So even if you use a pro make sure you understand exactly what they did and how they did it. Or better yet, do it yourself!

FOR MORE:
Internal Revenue Service, *irs.gov*
Social Security Administration, *ssa.gov*

Julia Anderson

LEAVING A LEGACY:
YOU DON'T HAVE TO BE RICH

"It is up to us to live up to the legacy that was left for us,
and to leave a legacy that is worthy of our children
and of future generations."

--Christine Gregoire, former Washington state Governor
(1947 -)

L eaving a legacy may recall images of wealthy people
donating big bucks to build a new cancer wing at the
hospital or fund construction of a homeless shelter.

Headline-producing check writing is part of the American
way. Bill and Melinda Gates are giving away billions. So are
Warren Buffett and Mark Zuckerberg. For the wealthy, charitable
giving is about do-gooder big heartedness and part of a long-term
estate-planning and tax strategy.

NEWS FLASH: Charitable giving is not just for the rich. You,
too, can leave a legacy.

The simplest way to be remembered is to put instructions in
your will to provide an inheritance for your heirs or fund a favorite
charity after you die.

But if you want to do good works before you fall off the tree
branch, consider a donor-advised charitable fund or set up a tax-
free 529 savings account for a worthy grandchild. Or do both.

What is a donor advised fund? These funds offered by
brokerage firms, banks and other entities, allow donors to make a
charitable contribution, receive an immediate tax benefit and
then recommend grants from the fund over time. In other words,

you can put money inside your DAF but still control the money, let it earn more tax-free until you decide when and how to give it out.

WHY DOES A DONOR-ADVISED CHARITABLE FUND MAKE SENSE?

You can accumulate money inside a donor-advised fund and let it grow tax-free. You decide when and how much money to donate to your favorite qualified charities.

There could still be tax benefits if you "bunch" your planned giving into a single year instead of spreading it over several years. The greater single amount could then be higher than the standard deduction in that tax year.

You get privacy with a donor-advised fund if you choose to anonymously have your fund manager send out your donations.

DAF managers typically offer you a menu of managed mutual funds where you can invest your money until it is distributed. These funds should match your risk tolerance and investment goals. Fund managers will automatically vet potential recipients as "IRS qualified" public charities.

The idea is to make charitable giving effective and simple. Contributions can be made when they most benefit the donor while disbursements can occur on a separate timetable – next year, in five years or even later.

Are there things to watch out for? According to an IRS warning, there are organizations that promote themselves as donor-advised fund managers but who are fraudulent. They are abusing the basic concepts underlying donor-advised funds by encouraging "questionable charitable deductions," the IRS said.

They also may offer what are illegal economic benefits to donors and their families (including tax-sheltered investment income for the donors) and management fees for promoters.

If these violations are caught by the IRS, donors will have the charitable tax deduction disallowed and face fines and penalties.

Make sure you are dealing with a reputable fund manager with a long and well-documented track record.

HOW ABOUT A 529?

A 529 plan is a tax-advantaged savings plan designed to encourage savings for college, trade school or other school-related expenses of any U.S. resident who has a Social Security number, typically a young person.

These plans are sponsored by a state or a state agency. Money inside these plans can grow tax deferred and be used for tuition, books, vocational technical schools plus a host of other related expenses.

Recent tax law changes allow money inside of a 529 to be dispersed for K-12 public, private and religious primary and secondary educational-related expenses.

Pluses for grandparents: As the owner of the plan, you control the account, including investment decisions and asset distribution. You can even change the designated recipient. Timing of when the money is distributed can be tricky because it can mess up Pell Grant and other scholarship applications. Check out all the rules. Leaving a legacy is important to many of us. There are lots of ways to do it.

Certainly, how we are remembered by those whose lives we touched is part of that legacy. You can give away assets by gifting your investments, retirement savings and real estate holdings to your heirs in a well-crafted will. Or you can assign them to a trust for a bank or other trust management service to supervise.

If you want to give something back before you die, consider a donor-advised charitable fund or a 529. You don't have to be rich.

FOR MORE:

"Leaving a Legacy instead of a Mess," by Suren Adams

5 Ways to Leave a Great Legacy by Joan Moran at HuffPost

4 Ways to Leave a Legacy by Bart Astor at Forbes.

"This is how you leave a legacy," by Jim Rohn at Success.com.

529 Plan Basics at Fidelity.com

IF THERE ARE MEN
IN YOUR LIFE

Julia Anderson

Demographic Facts
Speak for Themselves

An estimated 76 million Americans are part of the baby boomer generation born starting at the end of World War II until 1964. Davy Crockett, the Beatles, birth control, women's rights, divorce, assassinations and the Vietnam War are part of our experience.

Every day, 10,000 of us turn 65. The youngest will mark their 65th year in 2029. By then, 20 percent of the U.S. population will be 65 or older.

According to the Social Security Administration, women who are now age 50 have a life expectancy of 82.8, while men will live an average of 79.1 years.

That doesn't sound like much of a difference, but the reality is that women of this generation will likely be on their own emotionally and financially in their later years. Men, on the other hand, won't because they don't live as long, and they don't live alone.

Julia Anderson

WOMEN DON'T DIE. MEN DO

"The trick in life is learning how to deal with it."
-- Helen Mirren, English actor (1945-)

The numbers speak for themselves. American women outlive men. Meanwhile, women spend less time in the work force during their adult child-bearing years and generally earn less money over that lifetime of work.

For these reasons, American women must plan differently than men for retirement. The fact is that we often fail to do that.

Here's what the U.S. Census Bureau stats tell us:

- There are about 49.2 million Americans, 65 and older living in the U.S. The number is expected to double to 98 million by 2060.
- Meanwhile, older men (65 and older) are much more likely to be married than older women – 72 percent of men vs. 46 percent, women.
- Of those people aged 65 and older, there are 90.5 males for every 100 females. After age 85, the ratio drops to 58 males for every 100 females.

GET THE PICTURE?

Among women 65 years and over, the proportion who are widowed is 44.9 percent. By contrast, only 14 percent of men in this age group are widowed, while 73.6 percent were married and living with a spouse.

Conclusions: Men tend to die sooner than women. They live with their spouses until the end or, if widowed, find a new partner much more often than women.

The Census Bureau tells us that of Americans age 75 and older, an estimated 52.9 percent of women are on their own, while only 22.3 percent of men are single.

A healthy man reaching age 65 today can expect to live, on average, until age 84. A woman, on average, can expect to live until 86.6.

EARNINGS: MEN VS. WOMEN

About 73 million women are working and in the labor force (57.7 percent of the population). The annual median (half more/half less) earnings ratio of women who worked year-round was $37,118 as compared with median annual earnings of men at $48,202.

The female-to-male ratio of earnings for those working full-time, year-round was 77 cents for women to every $1 for men. This may not be job discrimination as much as it is job choice and hours worked.

Women tend to enter the "helping" professions (teaching, for instance) that pay far less than say an engineer working for Boeing Co. Women also tend to work fewer hours per week. Maintaining a household, caring for children and aging family typically are part of the lives of women, more than men.

POVERTY AMONG SINGLE WOMEN

Women live longer, but here's the disturbing part: The poverty rate among single women who are 65 and older is an alarming 20 percent, four times that of married couples the same age, according to census bureau data.

Why is that? Because over a life-time of work, women earn less, which means less money is being saved for retirement. It means qualifying for less in Social Security benefits.

Meanwhile, women live longer and will spend more than one-third of their lives living alone.

SOLUTIONS

Better financial planning would help keep the death of a spouse or a late-in-life divorce from becoming a financial disaster for women. To that end, every woman should have an Individual Retirement Account of their own, married or single.

They should pay off the mortgage, put money in regular savings for emergencies and stop giving the kids money. They should have the retirement planning talk with their spouses that includes what happens when he dies.

Meanwhile, we all are working longer to make up for the short-fall.

Of those Americans age 65-69, the percentage still working full-time has jumped to 30.8 percent as compared with only 21 percent in 1990.

FOR MORE:
  "What Works for Women at Work" by Joan C. Williams and
    Rachel Dempsey
  "The 5 Years before you Retire" by Emily Guy Birken
  "Prince Charming Isn't Coming" by Barbara Stanny

Julia Anderson

SIXTY AND SINGLE: MY STORY

"The kind of beauty I want most is the hard-to-get kind that comes from within – strength, courage, dignity.

-- Ruby Dee, American actress (1922-2014)

In grade school, I found playing with the boys much more fun than sitting on the cold sidewalk playing jacks with the girls.

Journalism, my chosen career, was (and is) male dominated. I liked that. I knew how to get along in that world. Smile but work your butt off and ignore the come-ons.

Mattie Ross, the feisty girl in *True Grit* is my favorite book and movie character.

At the daily newspaper, a full-time and meaningful career, deadlines and the competition to "get the story and get it right" all appealed to my nature. I was passionate about business news reporting, loved the scoops and the deadlines.

I didn't think much about how my life would go forward as I moved into my 50s.

Sure, I would 'retire' at some point but that picture was hazy. Married 17 years, my husband and I talked in general terms about whether we were saving enough. We decided that we were. End of discussion.

Meanwhile, we were building our dream house in the country, had a couple of horses, a dog and enjoyed vacations building an off-the-grid cabin in Idaho. I loved his parents and his kids and grandkids. He mine.

Things changed when the manufacturing plant where he worked abruptly shut down during the West Coast Enron Energy Crisis of 2000. Along with 360 other workers, he lost his job, just as we were finishing the dream house.

After a bumpy year, he found new work at half the pay and half the responsibility.

Within a few years, he began an affair with a woman he had met on that job and left me. He was 63 and I was 60. She was 43.

He took his horse, his trophy elk head, his pickup and a few pieces of important family furniture and artwork. She was nearly the age of his kids!

I did not see it coming. Neither did my family, his family or close friends.

STARTING A BLOG

I began writing about this wrenching emotional and financial transition at a blog I launched for women. I named it *sixtyandsingle.com*. There has been a lot to write about ever since: money, retirement, investing, death of spouses, Social Security, caring for elderly parents, Medicare, downsizing, budgeting. A lot happens in your 60s, single or married.

I have watched women friends endure the loss of a spouse to death and divorce. Two in my circle saw husbands die from cancer and another from Parkinson's.

These were wonderful, strong, intelligent, hard-working men, all dead in their 60s. Their widows are adjusting slowly, painfully...one day at a time.

A few years later, I remarried. Ken is a wonderful man who had lost his wife to ovarian cancer after a 28-year-marriage. We live in my house where we plan to stay until one of us dies or we go to a care center.

Marriage after 60 is different...the kids are grown, assets are separate, some of his friends and some of my friends have drifted away. Yes, we have a prenup, a tangible asset list for who gets what when, and wills that spell out how we want our stuff dispersed.

We are traveling, enjoying the moment while being mindful of the future. We know that everything can change in a heartbeat.

OUR 60S: PACKED FULL OF DECISIONS

As retirement looms, as we age, as illness may strike, decisions are made: Do we downsize? What about a joint household budget? Whose furniture is this, anyway? When do we quit the full-time job? Can we afford to quit? How much money and time do we have for travel? Should we still give money to our grown kids?

How do we manage the nest egg? Where do we get advice? You thought that you would just go on working. Think again.

When it comes to my marriage that ended, giving me untold heartache, there was little to my way of thinking that I could have done differently or now would change in that relationship. He just didn't want the life that I wanted.

Financially, I could have saved more or charged up more on my credit cards to balance out our assets in the 50/50 divorce agreement. But I'm a saver, not a spender.

My experience is not unique. Baby boomers still are divorcing at greater than average rates. It's not just men who do the leaving. A 70-year-old male friend was booted out of the house by his 70-year-old wife after 30 years of marriage. My friend just returned from a Mediterranean cruise with his new girlfriend.

The fact is that men in our age group who become single tend to find new relationships or remarry more quickly than women.

At 60, single women face unique challenges. Two friends who are financially secure are choosing the single life filled with travel, children and grandchildren. Another has a boyfriend, sold her house and started a new business.

FOR SOME THERE IS NO CHOICE: WORK OR STARVE.

Looking back, my transition in my 60s from full-time work to semi-retirement would have been smoother if I had thought about it more carefully. Retirement was this vague future without details.

In researching and writing for **sixtyandsingle.com**, I learned that many women are like me -- more engaged in the moment rather than thinking about what's next. I learned that many of us will be single in our 60s and financially on our own. For many that will be a hardship.

As another friend (a divorced nurse in her 60s) said, "I am still working full-time...it is not what I planned but it is what it is. I have my work and my grandchildren."

AVOIDING THE MONEY TALK

As for men, I see them living in a more compartmentalized world of work, of projects and staying busy. Men may avoid the money conversation, the estate-plan planning because it may remind them of their mortality. They often forget to bring their wives up to speed.

And, single men more than single women, want companionship. They don't want to live alone. To their credit most find comfort with women their age, women who like the same rock and roll. Some just want to feel younger even if the mirror and the Social Security card tell them otherwise.

FOR MORE:
"Get What's Yours," by Laurence Kotlikoff
"How to Retire, Happy, Wild and Free," by Ernie Zelinski
"A Single Woman's Guide to Retirement," Jan Cullianane

DIVORCE: OFTEN A FINANCIAL DISASTER FOR WOMEN

"You never really know a man until you have divorced him."

--Zsa Zsa Gabor, actress and socialite. (1917-2016)

At 54, she has been living apart from her husband for more than two years but has yet to initiate a divorce.

"I've got to get this over," she told me with a look of distress. "It's just so hard to take the next steps."

For her there are a lot of next steps: With a divorce can she continue to use his health insurance coverage? How does she negotiate a fair division of retirement savings assets? If he gets the house, what does she get?

Does she have enough money saved to pay for a divorce attorney? What does her future look like?

Divorce is horrible in so many ways...a personal failure, a loss, an emotional nightmare. For women, it also can be financial disaster. Few women are better off financially after a divorce.

The Atlantic reports that women typically see a 20 percent decline in income when their marriages end. The magazine called it "The Divorce Gap." Sadly, one in five women fall into poverty after divorce. Why? They likely have less income from a job than their ex-spouse and they typically have custody of the children. Meanwhile, few divorced mothers (only 25 percent) receive full child support as spelled out in their divorce agreements.

ADVICE FOR A DIVORCING FRIEND

"Above all be the heroine of your life, not the victim."

--Nora Ephron, American writer and film producer. (1941-2012)

A woman recently shared with me that she's been living separately from her husband for more than two years (her idea) but had not yet filed for divorce.

She told me she was going to Hawaii for a week with her estranged spouse where she intended to tell him that it was time to move ahead with the split.

It was clear she really didn't have the heart for it. But wow why wallow in that never neverland of guilt, worry and financial uncertainty? Turns out she's still using his health insurance coverage through his job. Going on a vacation together? Talk about mixed messages!

For me, if you don't want to live with someone, get on with it. Suck it up and carve out your own future. She didn't ask for my advice.

Here's what I would have advised, if she had asked:

- **Get off the dime and get it done**. The longer you dither the more time he has to find a new girlfriend, to decide he deserves more in a settlement and to hide money and assets.
- **Put together a post-divorce budget for yourself.** Add up your monthly cost for food, utilities, mortgage/rent, insurance, transportation, retirement savings, health care. This gives you a negotiating position in a divorce settlement.

- **Gather all financial documents.** Savings and checking accounts, retirement accounts. **Get an appraisal on your home** to determine how much equity is there.

- **Cancel joint credit cards,** immediately. His debt can be your debt and another negotiating tool in the divorce.

- **Open accounts in your own name** – bank, credit cards, savings.

- **Determine** how you will handle health insurance coverage, find your own or stay with his coverage?

- **Ask for short-term court-ordered rehabilitation alimony** if you have been out of the work force and are over 50. The alimony money will help cover retraining and job search costs. Some jobs in demand require little training. Among them, phlebotomist, paralegal, certified nurses' assistant. Don't expect much more than $15 an hour.

- **Horde your money.** Do you have enough savings to get you through the cost of a divorce? Do you have money to reestablish yourself afterward? Can your family help you?

- **Consider hiring a divorce team:** therapist/counselor, divorce attorney and a Certified Divorce Financial Analyst who can help you set up a post-divorce budget and help negotiate the divorce.

- **Stay married, if you're close to the 10-year mark.** If you have been married close to 10 years, consider waiting for the divorce until you reach 10 years, which makes you eligible to claim Social Security benefits on your ex-spouse's work record with no impact on him.

- **Check up on alimony tax reform:** The Tax Reform Act passed by Congress in 2017 made big changes to alimony tax rules. **The old rule**: Recipients (98 percent women) had to report alimony payments as income and pay taxes on the money. The payer received a tax deduction for the amount paid.

The new rule: The spouse receiving the alimony will NOT have to pay taxes on the income. But neither will the payer get to claim a tax deduction. Result: Tax savings for women, increased expense for men. This tax change becomes effective in 2019.

If you are at the beginning stages of a divorce, take time to do some research on what critical steps you should take. There's plenty of info online.

Check out WIFE.org where founders Ginita Wall and Candace Bahr provide financial planning resources for women, particularly those divorcing or widowed.

They also support Second Saturday workshops throughout the U.S. aimed at helping women through divorce and/or widowhood. Go to the website for information on workshops in your area.

Other topics at WIFE.org: How to Choose a Divorce Attorney, the Benefits of Being Married 10 Years, A Step-by-Step Guide to Preparing for Divorce and Life Events and Your Finances: Are You in the Know?

Buy their bumper sticker – "A Man is NOT a Financial Plan."

FOR MORE:
"How to Get Through Your Breakup and Create a New Life you Love," by Suzanne Riss and Jill Sockwell.
"Divorce: Think Financially, not Emotionally. What Women need to know about securing their financial future, before, during and after a divorce," by Jeff Landers.

WOMEN GRIEVE, MEN MOVE ON

"Well, according to the study, women actually don't want to get remarried as much as men do."

--Women's Health magazine

It's been nearly four years since a beautiful friend of mine in her late 60s lost her husband to cancer. He'd held it off for more than six years with blood transfusions and bone marrow transplants.

They had time to travel. They had time to plan for her life after his death. She seems to be in no hurry to start up a dating social life and puts a lot of time and energy into grandchildren and travel.

She went to Africa last year. She's now in Southeast Asia, traveling with friends. The other day she bragged about how she's gotten used to and now enjoys going to movies by herself.

According to the U.S. Census Bureau, a year and a half after the death of a spouse, 15 percent of women and 37 percent of men ages 65 and older were interested in dating.

Differences in desire to re-partner may stem from the different benefits men and women receive in and outside of a marriage," the U.S. Census Bureau says.

Widows, according to the report, are more likely to say they are reluctant to give up new found freedom and independence. Many perceive a sense of liberation no longer having to take care of another person, and value this more than additional companionship.

A friend of mine in her 70s said the men she met were either "looking for a nurse or a purse" and she would have none of that.

Widowers, on the other hand, tend to say that they have not re-partnered because they are concerned about being undesirable partners due to older age and ill health. However, widowers indicated that they were more prepared than widows to take a chance on a new relationship.

NEW RELATIONSHIP? TWO YEARS.

Census stats show that men are more likely to re-partner after losing their spouse; more than 60 percent of men but less than 20 percent of women were involved in a new romance or remarried within just over two years of being widowed.

And yes, remarriage is not always the only arrangement. At least one woman I know, lives apart from her special friend but travels with him. Others cohabitate but don't marry.

Single, remarried late in life or just living together, all require serious conversations about money, shared households, estate planning, tangible assets and investing for the long-haul. There are ways to manage it. (See my chapter on remarrying after 60).

Whether remarriage is on the table or off, a healthy love and sex life can always be an option, and studies show that both can also improve your overall health, says Tasha Holland-Kornegay, professional counselor in a Women's Health magazine report. "Don't allow past pain and hurt to determine your future."

FOR MORE:

"Remarrying After 60: It's all in the details," at sixtyandsingle.com

"What you should know before remarrying," Forbes 2016 online

"Why Men Remarry Faster Than Women After the Death of a Spouse: Women mourn, men replace," Melmagazine.com

---

MEN OFTEN IGNORE THE FUTURE. THAT'S A PROBLEM FOR WOMEN.

---

*"To the well-organized mind,
death is but the next great adventure."*

-- J.K. Rowling, British novelist, screenwriter,
producer best known for Harry Potter series. (1965 -)

S tories about women, men and money come my way all the
time. Here are a few.

SCENARIO #1

A woman lives with a man for most of her adult life – more
than 25 years. They never married.

First together in their youth, they broke up for a couple of
years before getting back together in their 30s for the long haul.

He dies in his 60s.

The long-time live-in girlfriend knew that while she and her
partner were apart in those early years, he briefly lived with
another woman. What she didn't know was that while with this
other woman he named her as beneficiary of his pension, if he
died. He never got around to changing that beneficiary
assignment.

Now, even though that old relationship is long over, the
former girlfriend collected a death benefit of more than $120,000
from his pension policy at his death.

His long-time live-in girlfriend of 25 years gets nothing!

Because they never married and because he never changed the beneficiary designation, there is no way to challenge this. The other woman's name was on the document. The long-suffering girlfriend's name was not.

SCENARIO #2

A couple, long married, plans their retirement and decides that they will start collecting the full pension benefit from his 30 years of employment. That's instead of taking only some of the monthly benefit so that the wife would continue to collect on the pension policy if she survives him.

He was in apparent good health, they wanted to enjoy an active retirement, so why not?

Within six months of retiring with the full pension benefit, he is dead from a massive heart attack.

She is left to pay her bills on her own without any long-term benefit from his lifetime of work and their shared life together. The pension payout dies with him.

SCENARIO #3

A couple had been married since their youth. A successful journalist and marketing guru, he launches a community newsletter in the 1990s during the exciting transition from paper to online news delivery. The newsletter was a money-maker.

Down the road, he is diagnosed with a blood cancer that slowly kills him.

Despite the dire illness, he persists in putting out the newsletter as if nothing is changing. He never talks with her about dying or about the details of the newsletter operation after he's gone.

While she had been doing the business accounting, he dies without giving her training in news gathering or in technical support for its online delivery.

She struggled to learn on-the-job while grieving his loss. It was a lonely, miserable transition filled with stress and anxiety. She eventually (ala Martha Graham) prevailed and ran the publication for many more years.

There's more: The newly widowed woman who faced massive debt left by her husband who owned a failing business. Or the woman who discovered unpaid mortgage debt left by a husband with a secret gambling problem. These men were in death denial. A lot of men are.

IGNORING LIFE'S CYCLE

In fact, Americans in general don't talk about death, estate planning, end of life issues or even the details of retirement. Experts say it's because few of us are ever exposed to death because we don't live on farms anymore where the cycle of life is always present. We don't witness death of family members because they are sheltered away in care centers rather than dying at home surrounded by loved ones, young and old.

When the topics of illness and death come up, we cringe. If pressed, men offer the pat answer, "we'll be fine," emphasis on the "we."

Men, more than women, do not want to think about getting old or about dying. That leaves many women picking up the financial pieces after they lose their spouses. It means many women "pay" for the mistakes made by the men who ignore their mortality.

Those mistakes might be:

1. Never getting around to updating beneficiaries on a pension plan or a life insurance policy or brokerage account.
2. Choosing to take all the payout on a pension plan rather than preserving half for a surviving spouse after they are gone.

Whose fault?

Men are certainly at fault for failing to plan for when they are gone. But women also get blame for not being assertive about estate planning, for not making sure that they will be financially whole, if their spouse or their live-in boyfriend dies?

If men don't want to talk about this, it will be a difficult conversation.

Talking about money is stressful, causes anxiety and can create push-back. But let's say you live with someone in HIS house. How will that shake out if he's gone and his kids want the real estate?

Is everybody clear on what happens if one of you dies?

WHAT TO DO, RIGHT NOW

Make sure beneficiaries on checking, savings, brokerage accounts are up to date.

If you marry or move in with someone after age 50, do you have a pre-nuptial agreement that spells out who gets what when you or your partner die?

On individual bank checking and savings accounts, put a POD (payable on death) name on the account. You can do it by filling out a form at the bank. The money goes to the POD beneficiary without the hassles of probate court or trusts. It can be your kids, live-in boyfriend or spouse. If you own an account jointly, the surviving co-owner will automatically become the sole owner of the account.

Consider setting up a legal living trust rather than a will to save time, money and the hassles of settling your estate in probate court when you die.

Here's a suggestion from Dr. Keith Ablow, a psychiatrist, author and nationally-known mental health expert: "If you do just three things in the next three weeks that you would do, for sure, if you knew you were going to die, you will improve your life," he says. "By taking this action, you will alter your life's course. You will be on the way to "truly living your life."

Many of us skim life's surface... work, kids, grandkids. It's busy-ness but not taking care of business. We make assumptions about the financial future and what happens when the man we live with dies. **Have the Money Talk!**

Julia Anderson

AS THEY AGE, MEN TEND TO MARRY YOUNGER WOMEN...A LOT YOUNGER

A therapist told me that some men have more trouble looking in the mirror as they age. One way to feel younger, more energized, is to hook up with a younger woman. Viagra makes that easier.

But there also are men, said my professional friend, who prefer the company of a woman near their own age because they have more in common with someone who has lived in the same time frame, who has similar experiences (maybe the death of a spouse) or who simply enjoys the same rock and roll.

From my experience, among over-60 men that I know who have lost their wives, all now are in new relationships. The good news is that at least among these men (I'm up to five and counting), they are remarried to (or hooked up with) women near their own age.

FIRST MARRIAGE GAP

According to the Stanford University study, in first marriages, men are near the same age as the women they marry. But, "the older men are when they marry, and it doesn't matter whether it's a first or a second marriage, the more years they marry down," the research said.

While the age differential is narrowing in first marriages, a significant portion of husbands are still substantially older than their wives.

In about one-third of American marriages, husbands are at least four years older than their wives, according to U.S. Census

Bureau data. Wives are more than four years older in just 7 percent of marriages.

The Stanford study proves what we've always known: The older a man is when he marries after 40, the greater the likelihood that his bride will be significantly younger.... whether the man is wealthy and educated or not.

Men in their 40s tend to marry women an average of seven years younger, and men in their 50s are marrying brides who average 11 years younger, according to the Stanford researcher Paula England. All we must do is look around and see how much younger the wives of men over 60 are.

A story in the San Jose Mercury News points to Dennis Kucinich, John McCain, Larry Ellison, Donald Trump and Larry King as a few examples of older men with much younger wives.

It's not just rich men who find younger wives. Men who marry in their 60s, hook up with women who on average are 13 years younger. Why is this a big deal?

It's because 47 percent of women 65 to 79 years of age are on their own, single with many still working to keep a roof over their heads. How many men in the same age group are single? Only 25 percent, according to an AARP Foundation study.

SINGLE? NOT FOR LONG

From my limited observations, men don't stay single very long. Three men I know who either lost their wives because of divorce or death have quickly moved on to new relationships. One is getting married this month, another has moved in with a girlfriend he met on the Internet, and another is "chatting" with a woman friend by e-mail.

On the other hand, most women I know who've lost a relationship spend time grieving, picking up the pieces, thinking about the meaning of life. Some are choosing to not date, preferring the rewards of singlehood.

Men don't do that as much.

Meanwhile, Millennials are narrowing the marriage age gap. According to the Mercury-News, the median age difference in a first marriage is now about 1.6 years between brides and grooms - much less than a generation ago.

That narrowing points to an overall trend toward more egalitarian marriages, argues Stephanie Coontz, author of *"Marriage, a History: How Love Conquered Marriage."*

"You're still getting a lot of guys who marry down" in age, Coontz said, "but I think that obscures a trend to more age-equal, more power-equal relationships," she said.

With both older and younger men chasing younger women, the law of supply and demand makes the marriage market a tough place for middle-aged people of both genders.

"For women, the market may be limited to potential husbands who are significantly older, because many men of the same age are interested in younger women," researcher England said.

From my experience, that's not true. Those of us who are 60 and single still look good to a lot of men. Plenty of men prefer the maturity of a woman near their own age...someone with whom they can talk with rather than someone who talks at them.

WHEN YOUR EX-HUSBAND'S NEW GIRLFRIEND TELLS HIM TO STOP TALKING TO YOU

"You gotta stop watering dead plants."

--Melissa Harrison, English writer. (1975-)

First some background. My first ex- and I married in 1968. We were from different cultural backgrounds and from opposite sides of the country. For both of us, the grass was greener.

After 13 years, two kids, the death of our second baby at birth, eight moves and a business failure, we divorced in late 1982. It was my idea.

I went on to have other relationships and a full-time journalism career. There was sorrow on both our parts, and anger about the divorce. But for the kids and because we cared about each other, we never stopped speaking. Until now.

Over the years, we've seen each other at numerous events for our children (two sons and one grandson). My ex- has been to my house, I to his for the holidays, for visits. Last year we spent several days together when he hosted a ski weekend for all of us (including my new husband) at his time-share condo.

In the past year, we've spoken weekly about our kids. Last spring, I bought a house from him so that he would be financially free to relocate closer to our older son and our grandson. His stuff is still in the house. So far, so good.

He's 73 and single. I'm 69 and married.

In the past few months he's fallen in love with someone who seems threatened by former relationships, including me, as well as his ex-wife from his second marriage that lasted 20 years.

Through a couple of abrupt text messages and a short-written note, my ex- is telling me that we now are done. No more touching base, no more conversations.

The real shock was at Christmas when he and his new girlfriend (who I've met...she's been married twice) returned a Christmas present along with a note saying, *"the past does not belong in our relationship."*

And further, he would "prefer to not talk about the lives of our children on a regular basis" unless there's something urgent. "I would prefer to talk directly to the boys when necessary," he said. "Thank you for your understanding."

Ouch!! This is from a man who has a generous loving heart, who has always included me in his thinking about the kids and who has been collaborative when it comes to helping them get ahead.

This is a 48-year relationship, a solid friendship. As the father of my children, I have always thought of him as part of my family. The best ex-husband that someone could have.

This banishment by the new girlfriend who is about my age feels mean-spirited, hurtful and controlling. Please, we've been divorced since 1983. Why should she make an enemy when she doesn't have to?

My friends wonder about my ex-. Why would he go along with this edict if he were in full control of his faculties? Maybe his recent angioplasty procedure did something to his brain, they wonder.

It is what it is. I see no option but to suck it up. If that's the way it's going to be, then so be it.

But will we no longer celebrate our children's birthdays together?

How about our only grandson...two parties....one with us, one with them? Who's going to write his obit or settle his estate when he dies? His kids, or her?

We live in a community property state. Has he thought about how a late-in-life relationship works when it comes to assets? (He's a medical professional).

Is she going to have him spending more money than he should? Hey, this is his life, but all this has implications for our children.

Darn it. This came out of the blue and really hurts. I've had friends drift away and felt sad. There have been other losses in my life that have caused heartache.

But at this stage after all these years there is comfort in the relationships that have endured. This was among them. I've always told my friends that I loved the guy, I just couldn't live with him. OK, I suppose the girlfriend has smelled that out. Who knows what he's told her.

Hey, even though I'm almost 70 and married, I'm being dumped. Don't we all have ex-spouses? Don't we still care? I do.

It isn't just me...he's not supposed to speak to his second wife, either. We've been banished to the waste land of the outer solar system never to be spoken of or spoken to, again.

Experts say, what you may remember most about a relationship is how it ends. After 48 years, this one is ending badly.

I was happy when I heard that he had found someone to share his life with. It never occurred to me that she would need to put

175

at stake through the heart of past relationships, those that have lasted a lifetime, until now. Maybe I am not the one to question this new relationship but maybe he should be.

Postscript: To accommodate my now 75-year-old ex-husband's plans to remarry, he requested the nullification of our 1968 marriage by the Catholic Church. It could have been handled better – he could have warned me that the church paper work was coming in the mail. He could even have written me a letter explaining why a nullification was important to him and why I should agree to the church nullification. He didn't.

FOR MORE:
"When men marry later age gap is greater," The (San Jose) Mercury News.
"What you remember about a relationship often depends on how it ends," - Marcia Reynolds, Psychology Today.

MEN MAY NEED SPECIAL CARE. DIVORCE OR BUY LONG-TERM CARE INSURANCE?

**"The dementia patient is not giving you a hard time.
The dementia patient is having a hard time."**
— from online Health Digest.

A friend recently purchased insurance that would cover the costs of their long-term care, if one or both needed it down the road.

In their late 60s, they already have sold their suburban home and relocated to a high-rise urban condo. His family has a history of Alzheimer's disease.

For them, long-term care insurance will protect their substantial assets. For others, it may provide an alternative to financial ruin.

But long-term care insurance is complicated, especially now that major insurance providers are realizing they miscalculated premium income vs. payout costs.

As a result, the industry is in flux, rates are changing, and new products are coming on the market. Bottom line: Long-term care insurance is getting more expensive.

WHO NEEDS COVERAGE?

Those who most need long-term care insurance coverage are people in the middle-class with total assets of $500,000 to $3,000,000. Why?

People with assets of a half-million or less will quickly burn through what money they've saved for retirement and then will sell their homes to use the equity. Once those assets are gone, federal Medicaid coverage kicks in to cover long-term care because they are broke.

On the other end of the wealth spectrum, those with more than $3 million in assets likely can afford to pay for their care without facing an income crisis.

Those in the middle face the biggest challenge. That's because if one spouse needs long-term care, those costs will drain away their nest egg. The comfortable retirement that they planned could be eaten up by care costs. The surviving spouse is left without enough income or savings to pay household expenses.

WOMEN ARE MORE VULNERABLE

Women have more reason to buy long-term care coverage than men since we may have fewer assets, but out-live our spouses. Basically, all the money goes to his expensive care, she has nothing left.

What to do? First, have a conversation with your family about the long-term care issue and how you would like to see it handled when the time comes. (Statistics say that 7 out of 10 of us will die in a care center or the hospital).

QUESTIONS FOR A FAMILY DISCUSSION:

1. If you needed care today, do you have a family member who would be the care giver? If so, have you discussed this with them as to how it would work for both of you?

2. Where would you like to have care provided? If you stay at home, is there a time that you feel you would need to move?

3. Have you communicated your wishes to anyone, if so to whom?

4. How would you pay for care today if something unexpected happened to you?

5. Are your assets large enough that they should be protected by insurance?

IS DIVORCE THE ANSWER?

While getting a divorce may seem drastic, I know a couple who married and then divorced but continue to live together in loving unwedded bliss to protect their assets in a community property state. If he became ill, he would burn through his assets but hers would be unaffected and vice a versa.

This may be worth considering, if you marry late in life and have separate assets. Or it may be one reason to not get married but just live together. Although after seven years, the law may consider you married unless you have a legal agreement spelling out your separate assets.

What is long-term care insurance?

Long-term care insurance has been developed to specifically cover the costs of care services that are NOT covered by traditional health insurance or by Medicare. These include services in your home for such daily living activities as bathing, cleaning, taking medications and food preparation, says the U.S. Dept. of Health and Human Services. Long-term care insurance may be right for you if you want to protect your retirement savings and basic assets such as a home. But there's a lot to learn before signing up.

SIX QUESTIONS TO ASK WHEN BUYING LONG-TERM CARE INSURANCE:

1. What is the size and reputation of the company selling you the coverage? **Recommendation:** Only work with large, high-rated AAA companies with a long track record.

2. Discuss in detail the range of coverage options and their costs. According to SmartMoney.com the average annual premium for the 7 million LTC policies in force is $2,100. **Recommendation:** Read the fine print, go over the plan. Ask exactly what the policy will cover and what it won't.

3. Will your agent put everything in writing that he/she is telling you? **Recommendation:** Make sure that what you hear is in the actual insurance contract.

4. Ask your agent how much he/she earns on the sale of insurance contract to you? **Recommendation:** This is not a touchy question. It's your money.

5. Does this plan allow policy rate increases? Has the company ever raised rates? **Recommendation:** Some companies have been losing money on long-term care insurance and have asked for rate increases of as much as 40 percent.

6. What is the length of coverage? **Recommendation:** Six years is a good minimum.

FOR MORE:

For unbiased research on long-term care insurance, visit the Insurance Division in your state for information and company ratings.

"Why Long-term Care Insurance is a Women's Issue" wife.org

U.S. Dept. of Health & Human Services: longtermcare.gov

American Association of Long-Term Care Insurance: aaltci.org.

National Association of Financial Planners: nafep.com

Northwestern Mutual at northwesternmutual.com

EVALUATING LONG-TERM
CARE INSURANCE CONTRACTS & COSTS

"Since there's no cure for Alzheimers, there no need to plan." **Fact: Planning ahead has real benefits.**

-- longtermcare.gov.

If something happened to you today— an injury from a car accident, a Parkinson diagnosis, a debilitating stroke, early onset of Alzheimer's disease – how would you pay for the years of long-term care that might be needed?

Or, what if you live into your 90s, are on your own and at some point, can no longer stay by yourself?

People 50 and over are asking these questions as they face retirement and make plans for living into their old age.

Americans can expect to live an average 78.2 years, an all-time high, reports the U.S. Centers for Disease Control & Prevention.

But what if you can't live on your own? The cost of a care facility, nursing services and even in-home house-cleaning and cooking services can easily add up to thousands of dollars a month. These costs are increasing at twice the over-all inflation rate, government research shows.

According to the Wall Street Journal, Americans over the age of 65 face a 40 percent risk of entering a nursing home for long-term care services at some point before they die.

A year in a nursing home now averages more than $40,000 and can be much more expensive. One year of care at home, assuming you need periodic personal care help from a home health aide (the average is about three times a week), would cost almost $18,000 a year, said a U.S. Department of Health & Human Services report.

Do you bet that your good health and good genes will keep you out of a home or should you investigate buying long-term care insurance now to avoid a financial meltdown later?

Single people, especially women, may feel most vulnerable because without a spouse or other family member to help, dealing with a chronic illness or the challenges of aging can get expensive. There may be no choice but to enter a care facility.

CARING FOR ELDERLY PARENTS

Because women are most often primary caregivers for elderly parents, they may be more likely to understand the difficult decisions that must be made about long-term care and related costs. For some, purchasing long-term care insurance may be the answer.

According to *longtermcare.gov*, a website managed by the U.S. Department of Health, long-term care insurance is designed to cover care costs, most of which are not covered by traditional health insurance or Medicare. These include services in your home or similar services in an assisted-living or nursing care facility.

Consumers ask these questions: Can I afford long-term care coverage? Or, can I afford to not have it?

Insurance industry experts say baby boomers with assets should consider purchasing long-term care insurance sooner rather than later as part of their overall financial and retirement planning.

While we tend to think that long-term care is for a person significantly older, a sudden diagnosis could change everything.

Candace Bahr and Ginita Wall, writing at *wife.org*, say you need long-term care insurance if your net worth is between $75,000 and $3 million. If your net worth is below $75,000, Medicaid (government assistance) will pay for your care as soon as your assets are depleted. If your net worth is over $3 million, it may be cheaper to pay for the care yourself when or if you need it.

Bahr and Wall suggest that those with a family history of chronic memory loss, liver cirrhosis, muscular dystrophy, Parkinson's disease, Alzheimer's disease, senility, dementia, or multiple strokes should consider coverage.

"If these diseases run in your family, chances are greater than average that you will need long-term care at some point," they say. The bad news is that if you already have any of the above symptoms or diagnoses, you may not qualify for long-term care insurance.

Typically, people buy long-term care insurance between the ages of 50 and 65. Costs go up the older that you are.

BUYING LONG-TERM CARE COVERAGE

The insurance industry offers a great deal of choice and flexibility in long-term care insurance coverage. Premium costs are based on the type and amount of services you choose to have covered, how old you are when you buy the policy, and the optional benefits you choose, such as inflation protection.

When shopping for coverage don't jump into a contract, say the experts. Look at the plan and all features. Some plans will provide monthly long-term care benefits as low as $1,500 while others will provide benefits of $12,000 a month.

Meanwhile, the long-term care insurance business is in major flux because some companies are losing money on policies that were sold at prices too low to cover payout costs. Manulife's John

Hancock has asked for a 40 percent rate increase to make up for the miscalculation. Others have stopped selling the coverage all together.

According to a Wall Street Journal report, the annual average premium cost is about $1,450 for someone 55 and older buying three years of comprehensive long-term care coverage with a $150-a-day average benefit.

For someone in their 60s, the cost for six years of coverage with an inflation option will cost about $2,400 a year. When building care costs into their long-term retirement planning, consumers may want to use some of their own assets in combination with insurance coverage. Price should not be the only factor in the decision.

Women, especially, often ask how much long-term coverage will cost, rather than what's the need. Since women typically outlive their spouses, their need may be greater. It's worth a family discussion.

QUESTIONS TO ASK:

Talk to several insurance professionals about what they offer before making this investment. Among the most valuable research websites is *longtermcare.gov*, developed by the U.S. Dept. of Health & Human Services.

Look for quality products and service. Deal only with companies that have a long track record. Research the premium rate history of the company.

Ask your agent for the percentage of claims paid by the company versus the number of claims filed. Share what you've learned your family. Determine what works for you and for them.

FOR MORE:
longtermcare.acl.gov
wife.org

Taking Charge,
Moving On

"When you're threatened, or something hard hits you,
acknowledge it, embrace it. Don't pretend that you
didn't get hurt – cry, think about it.
And then you let it go and try something else."

-- Teresa Heinz, businesswoman and philanthropist. (1938 -)

"Nothing can prevent life's tragedies. Grieve but have a plan," said Teresa Heinz Kerry, wife of former Secretary of State John Kerry, who lost her first husband, John Heinz, in a tragic plane crash.

As heir to the Heinz fortune ($1 billion), Teresa set up the Heinz Family Philanthropies. Among its notable goals is to improve the financial literacy of women.

For Heinz, the death of her first husband was "unthinkable." Dealing with the devastation of loss and at the same time struggling to make sense of a financial situation is very tough. Her advice: Make plans for unexpected events.

The things that create financial disasters are generally not the things we want to think about...the death of a spouse, a divorce, a serious illness, a disabling accident or the loss of a job.

So how do plan for them? The Heinz website suggests that women should become more financially independent. Good planning is key. It recommends:

- **Maintain files of basic financial information**. Be sure you have copies of all current assets; bank account numbers; safe deposit information; insurance beneficiary information;

IRAs and other retirement account records; tax returns going back seven years; mutual fund statements and copies of stocks and bonds; copies of health, homeowners, auto insurance policies; the lease or mortgage information for your home; copies of a prenuptial agreement; wills, trusts and powers of attorney; and copies of birth and marriage certificates. It is also a good idea to have receipts of major appliances in a file as well.

- **Have your name on all checking accounts.** If your husband dies suddenly, it could be very difficult to resume payment schedules if the checking account and home purchases are listed only in his name. If you are married, you should also open checking and savings accounts in your own name just in case a will is contested, or some other complication arises.

- **Establish and maintain good credit**. Good credit is essential to any sort of financial independence. Get credit in your own name through a personal credit card. Without good credit, it will be nearly impossible for you to borrow money to purchase a home or car, or even get a credit card, without assistance. Regularly check your credit reports for errors. Visit WISER **(Women's Institute for a Secure Retirement)** website at *wiserwomen.org* for more information, including steps you can take to establish and maintain good credit.

The Heinz Family Philanthropies supports *HeinzFamily.org* where women can find in-depth and useful information about **"How to Make Financial Plans for Unexpected Events."** The research stems from the personal tragedy of Teresa Heinz.

FOR MORE:

Heinz Family Philanthropies, HeinzFamily.org.

Women's Institute for a Secure Retirement, wiserwomen.org

Women's Institute for Financial Education, WIFE.org.

"8 financial tips for new widows: Build a team of trusted advocates and get your financial house in order," Forbes online

MEETING MEN THE OLD-FASHIONED WAY: FACE-TO-FACE

"When you meet people, show real appreciation, then genuine curiosity,"

-- Martha Beck, life coach, author. (1962 -)

When I was 60 and single, I spent exactly 30 minutes looking at online dating sites. I felt obligated to at least give it a try, you know, get with it... not to be so lonely or bitter that I couldn't at least envision some kind of future with somebody.

I never got past that first 30 minutes even as other women I knew signed up for eHarmony.com or Match.com, or some other deal where you fill out questionnaires, upload photos of yourself and look at mug shots of men arranged much like a police lineup.

Nope, online wasn't for me. In fact, I'd decided to go on living in my house in the woods because I really didn't care too much if I met someone. "If I was going to meet a man, he would have to come find me", I told my friends.

That's what happened. In the year after my divorce, a friend brought in some workers to clean up the old barn on my place. To celebrate the spiffed-up barn I hosted a "barn party."

Forty people including everybody in my newsroom were invited. We had chili, chips and beer. Country music on the CD player. It was a celebrated step into my new single life as a rural property owner.

Despite the rain that early November day, 25 people showed up including Ken - a man I had never met, although friends had told me about him. Widowed, my age. A guy who liked doing outdoor stuff. Friends invited him along.

Ken walks into my barn, mingles with the group and ends up at my house having dessert with everyone else. Before he left, he asked if we could meet for coffee. A few days later over coffee, we learned that we had plenty in common...books, travel interests, the outdoors, skiing and music. It went from there.

I would never have been open to this except that my friends filled me in. Ken had a good marriage track record. He had great kids. He was financially solvent. He had lost his wife to cancer after a 28-year marriage.

Soon, Ken and I were going on hikes, out to dinner and then dinner in. He had a float trip planned on the Colorado through the Grand Canyon that winter. Half way through that trip he sent me a letter delivered first by pack mule out of the canyon, then by regular mail. I sent him a coinciding letter that he received by pack train back into the canyon.

Two years from the day we first met at my barn party, Ken and I married.

HOW WE MET

My single women friends sometimes ask how we met.

"Friends." I tell them. "I trusted their opinion and their good wishes for me," I said. "We did it the old-fashioned way: Face to Face." It's been great for the both of us.

For the record, I continued to write at my blog sixtyandsingle.com. I've lived it. I understand the challenges, the issues related to money, work, retirement, Medicare, and investing a nest egg. All are relevant, single or married.

Many of us are in second, third, even fourth marriages. Many of us will likely be single again if we aren't now. The statistics speak for themselves.

I am focused on helping women with the myriad of challenges we face as we cross into our 60s, see our mothers become aged, and face retirement from jobs that we have loved. I am focused on helping women make their money last.

MEETING MEN FACE-TO-FACE

Elizabeth Bernstein suggests in a Wall Street Journal story that women must go out into the real world. "Become the designated photographer at weddings, bar mitzvahs and other events," she says. "Shooting video of Uncle Phil's 90th birthday requires you to wander around and talk."

Go to church, join a walking club or a choir. Ask friends for help. Volunteer at a fund-raiser or political campaign. Smile more. Why not!

FOR MORE:
  "Scary New Dating Site: The Real World," by Elizabeth
    Bernstein, Wall Street Journal

Julia Anderson

REMARRYING AFTER 60?
BE HAPPY. KEEP YOUR KIDS HAPPY.

*"Being someone's first love may be great,
but to be their last is beyond perfect."*

-- Unknown

My kids and some of my friends asked me why I needed to remarry at 64? The answer is simple.... because I want to. Because if I'm going to live with someone, I'm going to be married to them. Because I'm old fashioned. Because I like the statement of commitment that being married makes. Because I love the guy.

Married is the way I want it.

Having said all that, getting married after 60 (or after 75 as my mother did when she married Howard), offers some challenges...mostly around defining what's mine, what's his, and what's ours in terms of money, assets and debt.

So, over the past six months Ken and I have been working our way through the marriage planning process that involves a prenuptial agreement, term life insurance on each other and a list of tangible assets such as furniture, art work and other household items that would be distributed to heirs, if one of us dies.

Oh, sure - there's the party, the cake and the shoes. But, the not-so-romantic planning is intended to ease the burden on the surviving spouse when one of us dies, and at the same time help our adult children (three of his, two of mine) settle our estates.

What does a prenup do? It spells out what's his and what's mine in terms of real estate, separate debt and certain tangible assets, such as artwork and furniture. In our case, it also says that a surviving spouse can continue to live in our shared house until either they die or relocate. Then the house is sold, and the equity dispersed to the kids.

'REAL LIFE STORIES

Time out for a couple of sad stories. The first is about an unmarried 60-something Seattle couple who decided to build a new house together, a nice house, an expensive house.

He drops dead half way through the construction project.

She's left with an unfinished house and not enough money to pay for it on her own. His kids certainly aren't interested in financing their dead father's half of the project. She's got a mess on her hands.

The second story is about a 70-something couple that decided to buy a house together. Same deal. He dies, and she can't carry the mortgage debt alone. The down-payment money is lost, she's on her own, grieving for her lost partner, without a home.

Term life insurance policies with the surviving partner as beneficiary would have helped in these two situations where the survivor has no claim to the deceased partner's assets or money. We've set that up as well. The fact is you can buy a $250,000, 10-year term life insurance policy through several reliable online websites at a cost of less than $1,000 a year. That seems reasonable considering the alternative disastrous outcomes.

MAKING A LIST

The most challenging aspect of this is the tangible assets list. When you combine households, grandma's china can end up stored in someone's basement. Or that favorite piece of wall art from your childhood is suddenly hanging over your new step-father's fireplace. Is it tacky to ask for it back if your mother dies?

Or, from the surviving spouse's view, as in my mother's case, the daughter shows up with a U-Haul trailer and loads everything that was her father's out of the house less than a week after the funeral.

The lowest point was when she took the very bed that my mother had shared with Howard, replacing it with a ratty thing from the basement. The easy-chair from the living room that my mother had been sitting in went as well.

Whether you're in a second or third marriage, or have been married to the same person for 50 years, a list of tangible assets spelling out who gets what and when is a good idea. Even then, there could be fights.

PRENUP DETAILS

A Wall Street Journal story said that prenuptial agreements are becoming more common in second marriages and should be signed at least three months in advance of the wedding so that there's no possibility that someone was pressured into signing something at the last minute.

Each party needs their own legal counsel to review the document before signing. Full disclosure of assets is required.

With all these items checked off – life insurance, prenup and distribution list -- in place, we got married. There was champagne, carrot cake and a sing-along to the tune of "A Bushel and a Peck."

FOR MORE:
"Remarriage After 50: What Women, Men and Adult Children Need to Know," by Jane Hughes Barton.
"Marriage vs. Living in Sin After 50," at fiftyisthenewfifty.com

Julia Anderson

THE UNEXPECTED:
'YOU CAN GIVE IN
OR YOU CAN FIND MEANING'

*"While the experience of grief is profoundly personal,
the bravery of those who have shared their own
experiences has helped pull me through."*

-- Sheryl Sandberg, Facebook COO,
on the unexpected death of her husband. (1969 -)

By coincidence we sat next to each other at an outdoor barbecue. Our small talk quickly turned to the details of her life. She'd been on her own for four years after her husband's unexpected death.

"The first two years, I woke up every morning cussing his name for leaving... for leaving me with such a mess," she said, tossing her head back. "I drank a lot of tequila. Made some mistakes."

Now at 57, she's getting a handle on the challenges both financial and family. One step forward, sometimes two steps back, she seemed to be saying. Her husband had been a building contractor. During good times he bought mixed-use commercial real estate. The buildings are older with both retail and residential space.

"Everybody thinks I'm well off," said the woman. "They have no idea how tough it's been getting over losing him and figuring out my financial situation," she said. "And I've got a son who is addicted...I know he's stealing from me."

For her, there was a lot to talk about. I said, "Call the police on your son the next time he steals from you. It would do him and you a favor."

She nodded. "It's just been so hard," she said. "I'm alone so much that I go out to eat dinner just to talk to someone."

Lately she hired a property management company to handle one of her commercial buildings to get rid of a derelict tenant. It didn't happen.

"You pay people to help you out but then nothing gets done," she said. "I'm selling two of the buildings just to get rid of the headaches."

"What are you going to do with the cash," I asked.

She paused. "A lot is already spent on stuff I've got to fix at my house...maybe set up a bank trust for the rest I guess," she said.

I said, "Be sure to check out the bank's management fees on that arrangement."

She said, "I suppose so, everybody wants a piece.

Like many, she's struggled to sort out things. Her husband had overseen their business life and income.

"People just don't know how hard this all is," she said.

Maybe she could talk to a financial planning expert, I said, one who on a <u>fee-only basis</u> could help her put together a plan that would give her some long-term income.

"Ask your friends who might be someone to talk with," I said. "Make sure they won't try to sell you something for a commission. Make sure this is strictly for their best advice and nothing more."

FINDING THE RIGHT TRACK

We talked about how hard it is to lose someone who you relied on, someone that you loved and shared a life with.

I told her that I thought she was on the right track, and that things would be OK.

She asked my name and told me hers.

I doubt that I see this woman again, but I wish her well. Grieving and trying to get a handle on finances at the same time is not easy. Several women I know personally have gutted their way through it. I've seen them get back in the game and move forward emotionally and financially. One step at a time.

The facts are that 35 percent of marriages will end with the death of a spouse, usually the husband. Women will spend one-third of their adult lives financially on their own.

FOR MORE:
 "8 Financial tips for new widows," Fidelity.com
 "How to prepare financially for being a widow," USA Today
 "One woman's retirement savings advice," sixtyandsingle.com
 "Recent widows are in need of financial guidance," CNBC

Julia Anderson

MAKING THE BEST OF IT

In this section we explore recovery from the profound impact of loss. It's important since many of us will be on our own in our 60s and 70s.

We offer tips on solo travel and we dig into how best to manage our final years. In the section, *"Your body: what changes as we age,"* we focus on the physical aspects of aging, but we don't bother with weight loss, chin hair or varicose veins. Plenty of resources elsewhere on those topics.

Yes, our feet get bigger as we age, but so do our hearts. Yes, we lose people dear to us, but we embrace deeper, more compassionate love. We let go of guilt, of anger, embarrassment and trauma and forgive ourselves. Paraphrasing Stephen Stills' lyrics, we 'love the ones we're with.' *Making the Best of It* encourages us to set new sails, break new trail and look to the future with an open heart.

Julia Anderson

RECOVERING FROM LOSS

"I can be changed by what happens to me.
But I refuse to be reduced by it."

-- Maya Angelou, poet and author, (1928-2014)

"No husband, no friends," was the heading on an essay hosted online by The New York Times. In the piece, author Charlotte Brozek describes her ongoing difficult adjustment to widowhood after a long rewarding marriage.

She said, "Everywhere I go, everywhere I look, couples surround me in the supermarket, at the mall and in their SUVs awaiting a green light. I never noticed the twosomes before. Now they make me feel obsolete," she observes in her Private Lives personal commentary.

When her husband died a year earlier, Brozek said her friends "headed for the hills" and she became relegated to an occasional lunch date or shopping spree. She said her children want her to emotionally move on.

"Someone once said that being a widow is like living in a country where nobody speaks your language," she writes. "In my case, it's only my friends, family and acquaintances who all now speak Urdu — it's not the whole country. I discovered strangers possess more compassion than my own friends and family."

From what she shared in her essay, Brozek seems utterly confounded by the painful depth of her grief. She's equally surprised that some friends were not able to handle her new singleness or her pain. Then acting from despair and loneliness, she exacerbates her situation by selling her home and moving into a "tiny" rental eight months after her husband's death.

Grief counselors usually advise against such big decisions for at least a year. Brozek agrees that moving out of her house was an "idiotic" idea that sprang from a not well-thought-out plan during those first months of grief. She agrees that she did a lot of what she calls "wacky things" during that first stage, which she describes as "numbness" and experts call denial.

"Moving eight months after my husband died to take up residence in a tiny rental a few miles away tops the list," she said. "I sent most of my furnishings to auction and discarded the majority of the rest. Two days after moving into the bunker, I was reading with a borrowed flashlight because I couldn't count a lamp among my possessions. Everything I saved I didn't need, and everything I threw away, I had to replace."

Couples, she says, make her feel "obsolete."

UNPREPARED

Those of us who have been widowed (or abandoned) after a lengthy marriage understand how one can be caught unprepared for the total aloneness of this universe. Those who have yet to experience such a loss cannot imagine the singular devastation of being alone, how difficult the nights are or how tough it is to plan a schedule of activities just to keep moving and breathing.

A generation ago, those who were widowed turned to family or the church. Now children live far away. Church people may remind you of the world of couples. And you can only call "friends" so many times before you begin to hear from them how life moves on. But where is one's life going after such a loss?

There are steps and programs that can help with recovery, one day at a time.

A friend who was widowed three years ago found solace at *modernwidowsclub.com.*

The website offers relevant and empowering content from a diverse group of contributors of varying ages, as well as a monthly online subscription magazine.

"Modernwidowsclub.com reassured me that someone out there, gets it," my friend said. "It helped me get farther, faster with my recovery."

The goal of modern widows as described by founder, Carolyn Moor, is to establish local chapters where women can find support. (Find her video on YouTube).

FINDING SUPPORT

In her essay, Brozek, says she saw a therapist, a psychiatrist and joined a support group as part of her struggle to overcome grief. She puts her finger on the difficulties of adjusting to singlehood and how some friends can't handle the new situation and pull away. Every case including hers offers a unique path to recovery, she said.

In my journey, I turned to the death and dying research of Elizabeth Kubler-Ross who established the five stages of grief: denial, anger, bargaining, depression and acceptance. Can any of us who found ourselves suddenly 60 and single say that we occasionally don't revisit all these stages?

THE GRIEF PROCESS: HOW TO HELP YOURSELF OR SOMEONE ELSE

- Encourage expression of thoughts and feelings: "Do you feel like talking?" "I don't know what to say, but I care" "Please don't worry if you cry in front of me."
- Help create rituals. Recall good times.
- Help put regrets into perspective.
- Urge those who are grieving to look to their faith community and/or a grief professional.
- Consider a support group. Plan for difficult times/dates (anniversaries, birthdays, holidays, meal times).

- Help clean out loved one's things and use time for reminisce. Suggest writing a letter to the loved one or keeping a journal. Don't be afraid to have a good time or to laugh.

- Share favorite quotations, words of encouragement.

- Encourage person to take care of their health. Help shop, cook and write thank you notes.

- Be patient. Grief takes time.

- Avoid saying things such as "you should be getting on with your life.

- Sometimes, just sit. Suggested at griefandhealing.org.

FOR MORE:
Compassionatefriends.org
HelpGuide.org
Grief.com
Modernwidowsclub.com
Griefshare.org
National Hospice and Palliative Care Organization
Mayo Clinic, "Is Crying Required?
WebMD.com - "The steps and stages of grieving and grief:
    What happens."

TOUGH TIMES:
CRY WITH YOUR EYES OPEN

"Let me not pray to be sheltered from dangers, but to be fearless in facing them. Let me not beg for the stilling of my pain, but for the heart to conquer it."

-- Rabindranath Tagore, writer and Nobel Laurate. (1861-1941)

It's just going to take time. That's the last thing you want to hear from friends as they pat you on the shoulder over your loss. They've done their bit. They've given you all the comfort they know how to give and now it's up to you to survive one day at a time while the clock ticks and the black hole of grief surrounds you.

Well-meaning friends could do better for those of us who are newly 60 and single -- those of us who have lost a spouse to death or as in my case an unexpected wrenching divorce.

It is now 11 years since I learned that my then 63-year-old husband was involved with another (much younger) woman and told me that he "didn't think he could give her up."

I've come a long way from the shock and profound sorrow of that moment as I then lived through the divorce and into a new life.

In that first year of sorrow, it sometimes meant getting through just the next 30 minutes rather than the next week or for God's sake, the next year.

207

I had my episodes of plate smashing, of cursing the pain and crying my eyes out. Fortunately, I had a job to go that kept me from going crazy as things slowly got better.

I learned a lot that first year, I talked to a therapist, devoured books, pasted notes of encouragement to myself on the fridge.

On the advice of a grief counselor, I learned to cry with my eyes open, to stay away from people who wanted to gossip about what had happened, who looked at me like a specimen under a microscope. Keeping my eyes open meant the pain flowed out, not inward to corrode my soul, she told me.

ADJUSTING TO A NEW LIFE

Women are adjusting every day to a new life that takes their breath away. Adjusting to the profound aloneness of it, of the silence of the evening at sunset and of the constant inner dialogue as they plan the next minute, the next day, the next move.

A friend of mine told me that sometimes when she comes home to the empty house since her husband died, she immediately must go out again...to the store, somewhere. "Then when I come back the second time, I can handle the emptiness," she said.

Another friend who lost her husband has a grandchild living with her that has eased the empty house issue. But she too is early into the journey to find her new self.

She says she's looked at volunteering but finds many of organizations in need of stronger management. "I wouldn't be able to keep my mouth shut so I just move on," she said. I suggested that she might need a paying job. She nodded but I can tell it's too soon; she has more sorting to do.

Many of us in our 60s are too young to devote all our time to grandchildren although that option offers certain comforts. We feel that there's still a contribution to be made, a project to undertake, a problem to solve.

BEDSIDE READING

During my grief from loss, I recognized the two-sidedness of it. The pain kept me awake at night, but it also sucked me deep into the universe of mystery and discovery. I sought out authors that tackled the worst of the human condition.

Alexander Solzhenitzyn's *"Gulag Archipelago"* was actually a comfort.

Joan Didion's *"The Year of Magical Thinking"* about suddenly losing her husband to a heart attack enlightened me.

Authors Anne Lamott and Annie Dillard offer perspective on the human condition.

Viktor Frankl's *"Man's Search for Meaning"* explores the essence of human suffering and acceptance.

There's Susan Anderson's *"The Journey from Abandonment to Healing."*

"Thriving Through Tough Times: Eight Cross-Cultural Strategies to Navigate Life's Ordeals," by Deidre Combs offers ways to handle tough times when the people, health or bank accounts we counted on disappear, when we suddenly lose someone very dear.

WHEN "THE GROUND DISSOLVES UNDER OUR FEET."

So, how am I doing ten years after my crushing loss and disappointment? Friends would say I'm doing well.... remarried, traveling and working as a writer in semi-retirement. I still have private moments of inner sorrow over what happened. At *sixtyandsingle.com*, I share resources for those working hard to find their footing.

Julia Anderson

LIVING IN THE MOMENT.
LESSONS LEARNED

"You can order more than one dessert."

-- Nora Ephron, American writer and filmmaker (1941-2012)

When my marriage ended I fell into a black pit. I tipped over the edge and didn't hit bottom for a long time as my husband left, my best friend died, and I found myself on my own, worried, angry, and grieving.

This happened in the year following my 60th birthday when I celebrated with a big party, surrounded by lots of friends and family. What could go wrong?!

My relationships – marriage, friends, work -- had been reliable and mostly unchanged for a long time. I was into my 20th year at the newspaper. The marriage was going on 18 years. Friends and family were a constant. I was comfortable, proud of my accomplishments and confident of the future.

I write five years (now 10) after becoming abruptly 60 and single. My message is one of encouragement for those who are starting the journey out of loss and pain.

Waking up alone after years of companionship and the security of marriage sucks. In that first year of aloneness, I developed squirrel brain that had me up late at night watching absurd comedies rented from Netflix or listening to Garrison Keillor's *100 Pretty Good Jokes* on tape in the car.

I had begun divorce proceedings against my husband who had moved out and into a new relationship with a younger (much younger) woman. I attended the funeral of my best friend since the second grade who just had died of stomach cancer at age 60.

My husband and I had what I thought was a great life. My friend Sandra and I were only a month apart in age, knew each other's secrets, and knew each other's families. There was no way to replace either that marriage or her friendship.

RECOVERING FROM A TRAFFIC ACCIDENT

During that first year of being 60 and on my own, I described myself to others as feeling like I had been in a horrific traffic accident and that I was still lying bleeding on the asphalt. The ambulance wasn't even there, yet.

I drew heavily on the skills of a therapist who helped me through the heavy grief, mentally scraped me up off the pavement and got me headed toward the future.

My dreams were crowded, disturbing. Headless people, lots of yelling and screaming.

I leaned on friends who listened to me talk, cry and rage, then let me do it all over again. That first year of being alone, I covered my kitchen refrigerator with quotes from famous people written on sticky notes. Cards from friends, photos of my children and messages to myself from myself plastered the door -- a silent frenzy of over-lapping personal dialogue and despair.

"Tapping" exercises linked to acupuncture sites on my face became a morning routine. I chanted repetitive phrases meant to free me from the sadness, from embarrassment, shame and the anger in my life.

That first New Year's Eve, I toasted the coming year outdoors with my dog and a shot of tequila while smoking a Swisher Sweet. Burning kindling in the fire pit brought me comfort. Had I ever been alone on New Year's Eve? I couldn't remember that I had.

It sometimes was too hard to go home to an empty house, so a friend gave me the key to her unused but furnished rental. I went there after work, heated up a microwave dinner, wrapped myself in a comforter and eventually tried to sleep on her living room couch with the TV on all night. I was miserable.

I worked hard to just breathe. I pondered sunsets and talked to God as winter turned into spring and summer. I went on walks with my dog. This was my singular journey from loss to recovery.

Others have been on this journey.

A friend was left with a financial mess of unpaid debt after her husband died of cancer. Despite running her own successful business, she spent nearly a year fearing that she would lose her house. After repeated conversations with her bank, untold amounts of paper work, she refinanced, got her business back up and running and soon started dating.

Another friend was left to run her husband's online business after he died from a lingering cancer. He'd never gotten around to facing his approaching death or bringing her up to speed on how to manage. It took a while but now she's got it under control and looks 10 years younger.

I hated it when friends told me that it was just going to take time. That didn't help with the here-and-now pain or the monkey-brain white noise whirling at the back of my mind. Why had this happened? Why did I have to suffer like this? How could I have been such a fool to not see this coming? Why?

Abandonment is a tough one. That first year, my physician prescribed an anti-depressant and had me see her once a month. I read books on inventing the rest of your life. I read daily quotes from *"Each Day a New Beginning"* by Karen Casey. I recommend Susan Anderson's book, *"The Journey from Abandonment to Healing."*

At work, I began reporting and writing about women, money and retirement planning because I found out that many of us are not prepared financially to be on our own. I hosted 60 & Single workshops for women. I began writing my blog sixtyandsingle.com for women about money, retirement and making the best of it.

YIN AND YANG

Life after 60 is a yin and yang thing. More friends have died. The economy tanked, then recovered. Relationships faded. Children divorced. My sister became a crazy person.

Friends, meanwhile, introduced me to a delightful man who shared my passion for the outdoors and my keen interest in old stuff -- history, ancient civilizations. We began a relationship.

My mother (then 95) fell and broke her hip, made it through the surgery and into convalescent care and then to assisted living. That was while my bi-polar sister was attempting to become her guardian. After two years of wrangling and massive legal fees that issue was resolved. I became her guardian; the bank managed her trust accounts.

Mom settled in and was relatively happy at the assisted living center playing bingo, lunching with friends and watching TV football during in her final three years.

At age 64, I quit my full-time newspaper job of 26 years but continued a part-time career as a freelance journalist, financial columnist and Smart Money television host.

After two years of getting to know each other, my boyfriend and I married in front of friends and family. That spring, we flew to Peru and hiked the Inca Trail.

During that first miserable year when I was abandoned and alone, a friend told me I needed to "break new trail," create new memories and look to the future.

She shared a quote from the 20th Century French writer and philosopher Albert Camus, who wrote, *"In the depth of winter I finally learned that there was in me an invincible summer."* I meet women every day who are finding their own invincible summer, as I did.

FINDING THE RAINBOW
ON MY REFRIGERATOR DOOR

"When we learn how to say goodbye we truly learn how to say to ourselves and others: 'Go, God be with you. I entrust you to God. The God of strength, courage, comfort, hope, love, is with you...let go and be free to move on."

-- Author Joyce Rupp, "Praying Our Goodbyes."

By the time my divorce was final, the kitchen refrigerator door was covered with artifacts from my rapidly changing and disrupted life -- quotes to inspire me, photos, greeting cards. The arrangements were chaotic, haphazard, not unlike the life I was living.

At 60, I had expected to be drifting toward retirement, basking in the glow of a successful career and marriage. Instead I found myself struggling to understand what had happened.

The therapist that I turned to explained that older men typically leave long-time marriages for one of two reasons: Either the marriage had been unhappy for a long time, the kids are grown, so it's time to make a change. Or they look in the mirror and don't like what they see. A new, exciting relationship makes all the difference.

When he said he'd met someone new, it took away my breath. Blindsided me. It diminished everything about the life we had shared. It crushed my heart.

While this book is meant to help women with money issues, it also is about surviving. It's about working through the pain, the loss, the fear and the heartache of being on your own whether from divorce or the death of a spouse.

Below are messages to myself that helped:

– "We live in two worlds...the world into which we are born, and the other world that was born within us. Both may be a blessing or a curse. We choose." - Celtic saying.

– *"God Loves You"* from a brochure handed to me by a street person in Seattle.

– "Everything can be taken from a man or a woman but one thing: the last of human freedoms to choose one's attitude in any given set of circumstances, to choose one's own way." - Viktor Frankl, psychologist and author of "Man's Search for Meaning."

– "When we are no longer able to change a situation - we are challenged to change ourselves," Viktor Frankl.

– "I learned that true forgiveness includes total self-acceptance. And out of acceptance wounds are healed and happiness is possible again. - Catherine Marshall, (1915-1983) author of "Beyond Ourselves: A Woman's Pilgrimage in Faith."

– "You, God, must be responsible. You must have put it there. So, what do I do with it now? " - Catherine Marshall, American author.

– "If one is forever cautious, can one remain a human being?" - Aleksandr Solzhenitsyn, Russian author.

– "Age does not protect you from love. But love, to some extent, protects you from age." - Jeanne Moreau, French actress.

– "It is the friends you can call up at 4 a.m. that matter." - Marlene Dietrich, German-born American actress.

– "If only one could tell true love from false love as one can tell mushrooms from toadstools." - Katherine Mansfield, English writer.

- In the depths of winter, I discovered that within I had an invincible summer," - Albert Camus, French novelist.
- *"Luck is a matter of preparation meeting opportunity."* - Oprah Winfrey, American talk show host and multimillionaire.
- "If I'm too strong for someone, that's their problem." - Glenda Jackson, English actress.
- "If you wish to be free, there must be a sacrifice," - Biblical.
- "If I am faithful to God, he will never fail me."
- Question to actress Catherine Deneuve, actress: "You seem to choose to play women who don't win? Deneuve: "Maybe you don't see them the way I do. I don't think that the one who leaves and makes the other suffer wins, and I don't think the ones who are abandoned are the ones who lose."
- "It's never too late -- in fiction or in life -- to revise." - Nancy Thayer, American writer.
- "The way I see it, if you want the rainbow, you gotta put up with the rain." - Dolly Parton, American singer and actress.

Julia Anderson

'PRAYING GOODBYE' TO THE PAST

"A new set of experiences awaits me today.
I can perceive them unfettered by the memories of the
painful past. Self-pity need not cage me today."

-- Karen Casey, "Daily Meditations for Women"

My grandmother's secretary-chest with a fold-out desk top has been with me for years. Into the deep drawers of this treasured piece of brown furniture are boxes of stationery, family photos, children's school records, notebooks chronicling my work at the newspaper, divorce papers, mortgage refinance documents, my father's photo and obituary.

Compelled to hold on to things, I stashed a lot of stuff in this chest including a box with annual Christmas gift lists dating from the early 1990s.

It seems time to sort through the flotsam and jetsam living in grandmother's secretary-desk. Time to clean out and clean up. Come to terms with what lurked there.

HERE'S WHAT I LEARNED SO FAR.

After three years away from my full-time job, I can let go without regret. My work years were rewarding for the service the newsroom provided the community and the support we gave each other. But everything was changing about newsroom...the people, the business model. I can look back on a successful career with sense of achievement. That's it. All those work files went to the trash.

PHOTOS OF MY FATHER

My father has been dead for more than 25 years. I no longer remember how his voice sounded. There's no real sadness at his going. He had a good and rewarding life as a farmer, a public servant, a perfectionist, hypochondriac and worrier. He could be blunt, but God, I respected that man for his honesty, his one-liner wit and his commitment to the greater good.

The photos from his days on the farm with my mother seem like another world. Family photos, those vacations and treks to the mountains -- now sorted, labeled and stored. Maybe my kids will want them some day. Ha.

HOLIDAY REMINDERS

The holidays past, present and future are tangled. Old address lists and boxes of dated Christmas greeting cards must go. Saying goodbye to these reminders of change and loss allows me to breathe deeper and sleep better. I don't work too hard to keep up with friends that aren't there anymore. Divorce makes it harder. Many go away out of awkwardness or loyalty or whatever.

Even as new people come into our lives, others slip away. Two friends from 10 years ago are not in touch. I don't take it personally. They've both faced difficulties. Maybe old friends remind them of those difficulties.

In my desk sorting, I found reminders of friends who are lost, friends who are dead, family who have moved on, an ex-husband who left for a new life and a new wife. My father who's been gone a long time and my children who are no longer children but men with their own lives, their own challenges. Photos, letters, records, fading memories, notebooks – all this I can toss with a healthy, "goodbye."

"Sometimes we need to break a relationship, to bid someone or something farewell," writes Joyce Rupp in her book, ***"Praying Our Goodbyes."***

"It may be a marriage that has died, a friendship that is no longer healthy, a job that is gone, an old memory that has haunted us long enough...when we learn how to say goodbye," she says, "we truly learn how to say to ourselves and others: 'Go, God be with you.'"

In the burning pain of fresh loss this idea is tough to embrace. Forgiveness is difficult. Only lately can I say the Lord's Prayer without stumbling over the part where you forgive "those who have trespassed against you."

Maybe it's a matter of "tasting the darkness" so I can "see the real light," as Rupp puts it.

The lives we thought we would have were always an illusion. By now, we know life is about change. Soon, I may be able to give away the furniture from the past.

Four steps to praying a goodbye from Joyce Rupp:

1. **Recognize and acknowledge a loss.** Sometimes we're too busy to have that profound recognition.
2. **Reflect on the loss.** Find silence within yourself or a place of solitude to do this. Reflection is a vital part of healing our grief.
3. **Conduct a Ritual:** Light a candle or burn a goodbye letter to the lost person or relationship. Ritualize the goodbye.
4. **Reorient your life.** Come to terms with the loss and move on with an open heart.

Julia Anderson

"BY MYSELF" RESONATES WITH ME

***"I think your whole life shows in your face
and you should be proud of that."***

-- Lauren Bacall, American actress. (1924-2014)

Actress and author Lauren Bacall wrote *"By Myself"*, her autobiography, in 1978. I read it soon after at a time in my own life when I was in transition and was much more interested in Hollywood than I am now.

Her death at age 89 prompted me to search out the book from my library. I remembered liking "By Myself" 30 years ago. In rereading it, I still do because hers is a real story, honest, about her life from the time she met and married Humphrey Bogart in 1945, her life with him, her children and the ultimate crushing loss when he died of cancer in 1957.

But her story just gets started. Widowed in her early 30s, Bacall must find her way as a single mother of two young children and keep some kind of a career going (code for earn a living).

TURNING TO FRIENDS

She turned to her friends for support, some married, some not. Some reached out and included her, others couldn't handle her singlehood. Frank Sinatra had been a close friend of Bogie and became her close friend. But the relationship was on and then off.

Bacall describes what grief did to her early on. The desperate pain of loss, the slow realization that life alone was all about conversations with yourself, by yourself.

She writes, "People always ask what you'd change if you had your life to live over again. I wouldn't change a lot of the unhappy times because then I would miss something wonderful. But I would change like a flash--me during it -- how I behaved with Stephan and Leslie (her kids), either short-tempered or over-affectionate --avoiding everything I could that had to do with Bogie, with my past life -- my insane desire to get out of my house. As if that could erase anything."

This was the 1960s before support groups, online counseling and social media. Before ModernWidowsClub.com.

It was Bacall talking to her mother late at night, talking with her friends over dinner. Trying to find her way. It was tough. But this is no tear-jerker.

WRITING AS A FELLOW TRAVELER

Bacall writes in a self-critical way that draws you in as a fellow traveler. She looks back on her grief, her transition out of Hollywood back to New York, her recovery. She brings you along on a journey that is interesting for her candor about mistakes, about friends who dropped her and about men.

She marries again in 1961 to Jason Robards, among the most talented American stage actors of his time. Robards was an alcoholic, which eventually destroyed the relationship and resulted in divorce in 1969. From that marriage, Bacall bore another child. She accepted the end of that marriage as inevitable because of his drinking.

Bacall describes herself as a "risk taker" and went to Broadway first in "Cactus Flower" in 1965, "Applause" in 1970 and "Woman of the Year" in 1981. She won Tony Awards for Applause and Woman of the Year. In 1976, she co-starred with John Wayne in his last movie, "The Shootist."

Personal lessons learned: "The lesson of Bogie I had finally put into practice: In the face of inevitable, terrible happenings, how much better to hold on to one's character and hurt others as little as possible. The straight road," she said.

On who she was: "I've finally discovered," she said, "that you really don't learn from past mistakes. You do logically, reasonably, but emotionally, not for a second. I didn't mean to waste one more minute. Patience was still not my strong suit."

On losing someone you love: "The knowledge of death being part of life's cycle helps not at all. There is no way to prepare for the darkness of that pit of despair, that gaping hole that remains empty and gnaws constantly like an open nerve."

On working: "Work is essential to me -- really using myself, really functioning, body and mind at their best -- but it only heightens my emotional needs, it doesn't lessen them."

Bacall continued to write -- "*By Myself*" in 1978, "*Now*" in 1994, and "*Then Some*," in 2005.

On widowhood: "I had to get out from under being "Bogart's widow." That was not a profession, after all -- and there would be no hope of a new beginning unless I fought for one."

On being a single woman: "A woman alone can't win with wives. It's a problem I've had all my single life, and there's no way to fight it."

In the flurry of news about Lauren Bacall's death in 2014, there was little coverage beyond her Hollywood celebrity days or her marriage to Humphrey Bogart. The comments were about her beauty, her chiseled looks and smoky eyes.

Nothing much was said about her books or about her Broadway work. One-minute summaries don't allow for much. Bacall's memoir "*By Myself*," must be remembered for her storytelling, her candor as well as the rough patches and how she managed them. She finished her book this way: "*I don't like everything I know about myself, and I'll never be satisfied, but nobody's perfect. I'm not sure where the next years will take me--- what they will hold-- but I'm open to suggestions."*

Thank you, Lauren Bacall for putting a voice to what many women experience in the circle of life.

FOR MORE:
   Read Betsy Sharkey's piece in the LA Times, "Appreciation:
   Lauren Bacall's Voice resonated with Women."
   "Knock Wood," by Candice Bergen. Her memoir about growing
   up with her ventriloquist father Edgar Bergen.
   "The Year of Magical Thinking," by Joan Didion after the
   death of her husband.
   "Traveling Mercies: Some Thoughts on Faith." by Anne
   Lamott.

Opening New Doors, Breaking New Trail

Julia Anderson

WOMEN TRAVELING SOLO?
YOU'RE NOT ALONE!

"The more I traveled the more I realized that fear makes strangers of people who should be friends."

-- Shirley MacLaine, American actor and author, (1934 -)

Traveling solo was once only for adventure-hungry backpacking 20-somethings. Leave it to baby boomers to create a new and growing trend in the leisure travel industry: Seniors -- including many women -- traveling on their own.

Some are doing it for business such as the 65-year-old woman I know who has been in at least eight different countries on three continents in the past seven months leading training seminars for a U.S.-based manufacturer.

Or the 60ish mother and her 40ish daughter who just returned from three weeks in Italy, leaving husbands and children to fend for themselves.

A retired school teacher friend, Sharron, 69, joined a group of 35 on a Road Scholar trip (roadscholar.org) organized through her Atlanta church called "In the Footsteps of Christ," which took her to Jerusalem, the Dead Sea, the River Jordan and Egypt. Of the 35 people, there were only four couples...the rest singles.

For Cynthia Anderson co-owner of Sunshine Travel & Cruise Co. and USA River Cruises in Vancouver, Wash., solo travel and women-only group travel have been among the biggest surprises in their industry's growth over the past 10 years.

That's good news for single women as well as for those who are married but whose spouse doesn't travel.

Anderson said women travelers once represented about 20 percent of USA River Cruise business, but that percentage has climbed to 37 percent.

"We're seeing a huge surge of people wanting to take family and extended-family members on trips," she said. "We're seeing many in the 55-and-older age group who are opting for small ship travel. Women love them because when you're on a ship of say 28 passengers somewhere in the world. You end up knowing everybody and it feels safe."

Inter-generational travel, especially grandmothers and their grandchildren, is another growing category.

WHAT WOMEN TRAVELERS WANT

April Merenda, president and co-founder of the website *gutsywomentravel.com*, explains that single women travelers want a unique travel experience.

"First, single women travelers don't want couples...they don't want to feel like a fifth wheel," Merenda said. "Secondly, they like to linger, ask questions and multi-task. That may mean getting a spa treatment, attending a cooking class, shopping or hearing a guest educator."

Couples, she said go to resorts and tend to concentrate on one location. Single women are looking for variety, interesting experiences and bonding with other women.

"Women like the company of like-minded women," Merenda said. "There's strength in numbers. They will share what's happening in their lives be it aging parents or teenage grandkids."

Merenda, who founded her online travel business for women more than 10 years ago, said the number of women who are traveling completely on their own without other family or friends has jumped from about 50 percent of her clients to 70 percent.

"Gutsy Women is not about climbing Mount Everest," she said, "but about having the courage to put yourself first."

"Women spend their lives doing for others," she said. "Independent travel is about occasionally making time for yourself to refresh and renew your mind, spirit and body in the company of like-minded women at fascinating destinations."

SAFE BUT SINGLE

Gutsywomentravel.com and travel and tour businesses like it catering to solo travelers emphasize the safety features of their tours and are typically designed to offer a variety of experiences and chances to meet local people.

At *gutsywomentravel.com*, trips are no more than seven days' duration or less "as we recognize that women are time-deprived," Merenda said. Women-only tour groups and the travel industry in general recognize growing market opportunities by catering to women, since women make 70 percent of all travel decisions.

U.S. Travel Association data:

40.3 million Americans are age 65 and older. Of those about 23 million are women with 59 percent married and 41 percent single. Of the 17.4 million men, 65 and older, 71 percent are married, 29 percent, single.

In addition to a growing number of solo travelers, more couples are taking separate vacations, Merenda said.

"Couples may have differing vacation schedules... she may take a vacation alone because he may be working or have different interests," she said. "She can do a cooking class in France and he doesn't mind because she's in the safety of like-minded women."

INTER-GENERATIONAL TRAVEL

At Road Scholar, a not-for-profit Boston-based travel and learning organization, the trends show an increase in international travel and intergenerational travel.

"Our programs have always offered accommodations for single travelers," said Stacie Fasola, Road Scholar director of public relations "Our only barrier is ability level in terms of walking, hiking. Our programs are rated accordingly."

Road Scholar encourages solo travelers to share double-occupancy rooms. It charges extra -- in the $200 to $650 per person range -- for a single room.

Fasola said a typical Road Scholar traveler is a retired female educator who may have been a school administrator or librarian. About 60 percent of Road Scholar clients are women who like the educational aspects of travel.

EATING ALONE? NOT

"Our solo travelers may have concerns about safety," Fasola said. "They likely will not want to eat alone or go to hotels alone. Travel is an experience you want to share. We help make that happen."

At Rick Steves' Seattle-based tour operator and guide publishing company, a growing trend is not solo women travelers, but male solo travelers, said Deanna Woodruff, tour department manager.

"In 2000, we occasionally had a solo male on one of our tours," she said. "Now it is common to have at least one solo male traveler on each tour and on some tours, you may find two or three."

TRAVEL WEBSITES:
cruiseandresorts.com
gutsywomentravel.com
roadscholar.org
ricksteves.com
tripadvisor.com
solotravelerworld.com

Tips for traveling on your own:

1. Use a quality travel agency or travel company with a solid track record to book your trip. Online prices may look good but can be misleading or a scam.

2. Do your homework. Get reliable recommendations on travel agents and tour agencies.

3. When comparing trip prices make sure they are apples-to-apples trip comparisons.

4. Go on a trip with an open mind. You will return with new friends and memories from life-changing experiences.

5. Small group travel means that you're not alone but have security and a travel director to assist you.

6. Share your goals with your travel director. If you want a camel ride, say so.

7. Take lots of small denominations in foreign currency to avoid international ATM fees and tipping awkwardness when traveling solo.

8. Never allow a hotel desk clerk to verbally mention your room number when you check in. Instead have them write it down, then look at the number when you're on the elevator.

9. Don't put off your travel dreams because you're on your own. Consider your options and prices. Go with like-minded women. Make something happen.

Julia Anderson

VOLKSSPORTING:
GET OUT AND SEE THE WORLD!

"An early-morning walk is a blessing for the whole day."
-- Henry David Thoreau (1817-1862)

"The best remedy for a short temper is a long walk."
-- Jacqueline Schiff (1985-)

VOLKSSPORTING

WHAT: Noncompetitive organized walking.

STARTED: Germany 1968.

TODAY: Volkssporting clubs exist in 40 countries.

U.S. ASSOCIATION: American Volkssport Association.

U.S. MEMBERSHIP: 250 chartered clubs.

MISSION: To promote and organize walking and other noncompetitive events that encourage physical fitness, fun and friendship.

WEBSITE: *www.ava.org* for club listings, new walker's packets.

Julia Anderson

On any given day, Joe Titone, Vancouver, Wash. is out for a walk. As president of the All Weather Walkers Volkssport club in Vancouver, Titone helps organize noncompetitive walking events for his 45 club members.

"Walking is a healthy activity...we just give it a bit of organization to get people seeing new parts of our area," Titone said. "And there's the great social aspect to it."

Titone's favorite walks are inside Portland, Ore.'s Forest Park and a trail around the lower end of Lacamas Lake at Round Lake near Camas, Wash.

All Weather Walkers is part of a national and international phenomenon known as volkssporting that began in Germany in 1968. In the U.S., volkssporting involves 250 clubs that sponsor 3,000 walking events a year.

These events are non-competitive for speed or distance, but members of the American Volkssport Association may choose to record points toward Achievement Award incentives using an AVA journal.

For Jan Veeder, volkssport walking is about healthy exercise and meeting people. As a member of the Border Crossers, a Longview, Wash. group, Veeder does local walks but also likes stepping out for regional events around the Pacific Northwest. She fondly remembers meeting friends for a weekend of walking in the Columbia Gorge.

"You don't have to worry about whether it is a safe place to walk or what the terrain will be like," said Veeder, 69 and widowed. "The real appeal is meeting people. It's incredible."

According to the American Volkssport Association, nearly 400,000 people took part in AVA events during a recent two-year period.

Someday, Veeder would like to make a volkssport event part of a trip to Europe where thousands of enthusiastic walkers turnout to explore such locations as the Irish countryside or Italy's Cinque Terre coastline.

INTERNATIONAL WALKS

Walking Adventures International offers volkssport walking-travel opportunities in all 50 states and 58 countries on seven continents. The company's Great Circle Route provides guided walking tours in the United Kingdom and Europe that "explore history, gardens, culture and natural wonders along the trails."

FOR MORE:
ava.org
esva.org
walkingadventures.com

TRAVELING WITH GRANDCHILDREN

"Young children are wonderful tourists, if you gear the trip to their interests rather than yours."

-- Deborah Jacobs, *"Seven Tips for Traveling with Grandchildren"*

N o parents, a few snacks, and a phone app or two. Grandparents traveling with grandchildren --- it's a big and growing travel trend.

And why not?!! Baby boomer retirees over 60 are more active than prior generations.

They have the time and resources along with a sense of worldly adventure that has them looking for shared experiences with our grandkids.

That's especially true if the grandkids live in another city and there's not much time for one-on-one time together.

Traveling without the "middle layer" of parents as one travel writer described it, creates a strong bond between grandparents and their grandchildren.

When I got the green light to take my 10-year-old grandson, Jason, to Disney World, I immediately booked tickets. Our six days together was a great experience.

We screamed together on the Rock n Roller Coaster and The Twilight Zone Tower of Terror. We shared meals, scrambled for restrooms and hurried together to catch planes and buses

We held hands in the wave pool at Typhoon Lagoon where I got smacked in the eye by a body surfer. We raced to get on the Seven Dwarfs Mine Train in the Magic Kingdom and got out just in time for the fireworks. In all, we were on 12 roller coasters plus waterslides.

MY GOALS: HAVE FUN AND GET CLOSER TO MY GRANDCHILD

That all happened for sure. We had time over meals to talk.

There also was time apart. The lodge pool and the water park were the easiest with life guards posted everywhere. He played with other kids. One night he stayed in the room with his iPad while I went in search of a martini.

On our flight home we talked about travel tips for grandparents and grandchildren traveling together. Here's what we came up with:

Jason's tips:

- Carry a small backpack with extra socks, water bottles and few snacks. Granola bars and pretzels worked for us. Be prepared for bad weather. We were caught in a thunder storm at Typhoon Lagoon. Have a rain poncho for emergencies.
- Go to the bathroom before you get on the airplane. Go to the bathroom as often as possible. Buy the smart phone app "Heads Up" to play while standing in ride waiting lines. We played with another family in line. It was fun.
- Always have something to read. The iPad Star Wars game came in handy. Bring Band-Aids and mole skin for any blistered toes from all the walking.
- If you're going to be at a pool, be sure to bring a face mask (they didn't let me use the snorkel) and/or swim goggles. Have plastic bags for the wet clothes.

Grandma's tips:

- If your grandchild is under age...have signed travel documents from the parents and a photo ID from his school. My documents included emergency medical permission from his parents, travel permission and his birth certificate.
- Meet with your grandchild's parents to explain the trip. Ask about their rules regarding TV, food or spending money and how you will stay in touch.
- If an iPad is along, set rules with the grandchild for how and when it is turned on. Set clear expectations about acceptable behavior...no talking back. Bring along a favorite stuffed animal or pillow good for sleeping on planes. (age 10)
- Plan for some time apart....in the pool or in a supervised play area. A video game room came in handy on our last morning while we waited for our bus to the airport.
- Take lots of photos for a trip scrapbook. Memories are important.

Disney World tip:

- Download the Disney World app to your iPhone and use it to sign up for Fast Passes to the most popular rides.

Top Destinations:

- Orlando, Fla., Italy, Mexico, Costa Rica, Hawaii, England.

FOR MORE:
roadscholar.org
grandparents.com
smithsonianjourneys.org

Julia Anderson

Your Body:
What Changes As You Age

Gerontology - The study of the social, psychological and biological aspects of aging. Gerontologists may include researchers and practitioners in many fields -- biology, medicine, nursing, dentistry, social work, physical and occupational therapy.

Geriatrics - The department of medicine dealing especially with aging and diseases of the elderly.

THE AGING PROCESS:
WHAT TO EXPECT. HOW TO MANAGE.

"And the beauty of a woman
with passing years only grows."

-- Audrey Hepburn, American actress (1929-1993).

According to Dean Anderson, writing at Sparkpeople.com, only 32 percent of adults 65 and older follow a regular exercise plan, and for those 45 to 64, the number is even lower at 30 percent.

Regular exercise is the easiest way to stay mentally and physically fit as we grow older, says Dr. William Hazzard M.D., an expert on aging in America.

For more than 40 years, Dr. Hazzard, a retired Seattle physician and researcher, has been studying the aging process. His medical textbook, *"Principles of Geriatric Medicine and Gerontology"* is the go-to resource for physicians worldwide who are in advanced training for the care and treatment of patients in the last phases of their lives.

The book also serves as a resource for primary care doctors, internists and others who may need "instant" information for how to treat an older patient.

"People become more complex to manage as they age," Hazzard told me. "That diversity of care increases rather than decreases as we age. Ideally our care as we age is a team effort with the patient's needs and welfare at the center of the discussion."

Now in its sixth edition, *"Principles of Geriatric Medicine"* first appeared in 1984 as Hazzard built the gerontology teaching program at the University of Washington School of Medicine in Seattle

Later, he became vice department chairman at Johns Hopkins University Medical School in Baltimore where he helped establish a Center on Aging and Health. He then spent four years at Wake Forest University in North Carolina as chairman of the Department of Medicine infusing geriatrics training throughout the school. In retirement, Dr. Hazzard serves as professor emeritus at the UW and continues to share his knowledge and views on aging.

WHAT WE SHOULD KNOW

What does Dr. Hazzard say about aging? He describes the human organism as extremely complicated, which on the surface, functions well for most of us into our 70s.

"We (physically) peak rather early in our 20s, maybe 30s," he said. "But there's a long period of middle age from 25 to 75 where there's a gradual decline in physiology but an increase in knowledge and experience that we mostly take for granted."

We can remain in good health and stay fit into our 60s, he says, if we stay active, don't smoke or drink too much and have good genetics.

However, as we enter our late 60s and mid-70s, aging may start to break through.

"The closer we get to the end, we may face a crisis such as a stroke, heart attack, a fall or Alzheimer's that changes things," he said.

In geriatric terms, Dr. Hazzard said these crisis points are not diseases but syndromes that make us more vulnerable.

"At age 85, you don't cure heart disease, you manage it," he says. "We all become more complex and our (health) management becomes more complex."

Dr. Hazzard says that even though there's been great progress in understanding how the human body ages, researchers and physicians are only beginning to recognize the trade-offs in treatment of certain syndromes in the elderly.

For example, should a physician try to lower his elderly patient's blood pressure with medication to a level that's normal for a 50-year-old? Maybe not, he says.

"We know that systolic blood pressure goes up as almost a natural part of the aging process," Hazzard said. "What's the optimal blood pressure in a 75 or 85-year-old?"

MORE VULNERABLE TO OUR GENETIC WEAKNESSES

Ideally, he said, we find a physician who we can grow old with, who will be the captain of our care team...a physician who is sensitive to the complexities of aging and who will listen to us. Preventive care is a key part of our management program because as we age we become more vulnerable to our genetic weaknesses in terms of heart disease, Alzheimer's or stroke.

"As a geriatric physician, you've really got to love old people," Hazzard said. "Women tend to be more gifted in that, more sensitive. She (the doctor) may have had a personal experience with a grandmother or other family member that created a positive experience."

How do we find a physician with geriatrics training? Using the Internet to search for doctors certified in geriatrics at AgingCare.com. Make an appointment and do an interview. You want someone who will listen and be your advocate.

Dr. Hazzard sees geriatrics as the opposite of most subspecialties in medicine. Instead of narrowing a doctors' expertise to a specialty such as oncology, doctors trained in geriatrics must be knowledgeable in many areas intended to help older people remain mentally healthy, mobile and independent.

This holistic approach doesn't just treat current medical conditions but looks at family history with an eye to prevention or to developing a program to support the aging person as they become frail.

A doctor trained in geriatrics will help devise a "healthy aging plan" for you. The goal, Hazzard said, is not to try to have everyone live to 100, but to work to "preserve respect, dignity and comfort" for patients as they age. His message to healthy 65-year-olds? "Keep running and keep reading."

FOR MORE:
womenshealth.gov
sparkpeople.com
Gerontological Society of America, geron.org
"Younger Next Year," by Chris Crowley and Henry Lodge, M.D.

TIPS FROM MAYO CLINIC:

1. Stay active with daily physical exercise.
2. Eat a healthful diet.
3. Don't smoke.
4. Get adequate amounts of calcium and vitamin D.
5. Maintain a healthy weight.
6. Be social.
7. Stay mentally active

MANAGING STRESS:
FORGET THOSE WALKS ON THE BEACH

"We must have a pie.
Stress cannot exist in the presence of a pie."

-- David Mamet, American author and screenwriter. (1947 -)

H ere's a rundown from my friendship circle of 60-something women.

A single-woman friend moved out of her suburban Atlanta home after living there 40 years and turned it over for foreclosure. She's now in an apartment surviving on a teacher's pension.

Another has a husband who is deteriorating from Parkinson's disease. Still another is in counseling with her 70-year-old bi-polar husband who stopped taking his medication and is making life miserable for everyone.

Another, widowed three years, has fallen in love. She's excited, trying to take it one day at a time as she gets to know this person and explores a possible future with him.

Another is dealing with the recent death of her mother-in-law. Will she and her husband continue to live in their home or -- according to a well-planned inheritance -- will they move into the much larger home of the parents?

Another is celebrating her husband's retirement from a successful 45-year career. As she said goodbye to us at the front door after the retirement party, she mentioned with some anxiety, "he doesn't know how I spend my day...that I have a quiet cup of coffee in the morning, read and really get started on things after lunch. There will be big changes around here with him home."

A 60-something friend moved her 93-year-old mother from Florida to Detroit where she lives. The next challenge: Rehabilitate her mother who has had a bad stroke, so she can eat on her own.

OUR COMPLICATED 60S

Life in our 60s -- everything gets more complicated – marriages, parents, kids. Forget those financial planning brochure cover photos that have you strolling hand-in-hand on a beach with your good-looking silver-haired spouse. Who has time for that?

Many of us have parents who are living longer. Husbands are retiring. Others have died. Some have moved on without us. Never mind everything going on with our kids, grandkids. Life just keeps happening. Maybe this shouldn't be a surprise, but it is.

Was life this complex for my mother? Not exactly. She lived in the same town as her mother. She lived in the same house for 70 years. She was married to the same man for 51 years before my dad died at 80. None of this was true for me. The good news is that my blood pressure doesn't seem to be higher than my mother's was at the same age.

Stress warning signs: Memory problems. Inability to concentrate. Poor judgment. Seeing only the negative. Constant worrying. Irritability or short temper. Feeling overwhelmed. Sense of loneliness and isolation.

Aches and Pains. Chest pain, rapid heartbeat. Loss of sex drive. Eating too much or not enough. Isolating yourself from others. Using alcohol (cigarettes, drugs to relax).

According to **helpguide.org,** how much is too much varies from person to person. "Stress-hardy people have an optimistic attitude," says HelpGuide. "They tend to embrace challenges, have a strong sense of humor, accept that change is part of life, and believe in a higher power or purpose."

TIPS FOR MANAGING STRESS:

- **Become a problem-solver.** Decide which problems in your life are solvable and which are beyond your control. "Learn how do calmly look at a problem, think of possible solutions," they recommend. "Sometimes it's not worth the issue to argue. Think ahead about how you will spend your time. Make a to-do list, set priorities and do those things first.

- **Relax.** Take deep breaths. Stretch. Massage tense muscles. Take time to do something that you want to do.

- **Take care of your body.** Get enough sleep. Eat right and avoid dealing with stress in unhealthy ways such as drinking wine into the evening.

- **Exercise.** It's a miracle to me that exercise can make a huge difference in my mood and sense of well-being.

- **Connect with others.** Among my most valuable relationships is one with a group of five women who meet monthly for coffee to share life's challenges. Going on 12 years.

- **Consider professional counseling.**

- **Short-term use of an antidepressant** or an anti-anxiety medication may be needed. Some friends swear by yoga.

During the worst of my divorce crisis, I used "tapping" to stay in the moment and avoid over-whelming despair. The idea is to create a mantra of forgiveness and tap your body with your hand as you silently repeat the mantra. It worked.

FOR MORE:

"The Journey from Abandonment to Health," by Susan Anderson

"Man's Search for Meaning," by Viktor Frankl

"Beyond Ourselves," by Catherine Marshall

"Each Day a New Beginning," Daily Meditations for Women

"Tapping for Forgiveness," with Julie Schiffman on YouTube

HOARDING:
MORE TEMPTING AS WE AGE

"Your home is living space, not storage space."

-- Francine Jay, author of the "Joy of Less."

A friend sent me a review of *"Dirty Secret,"* a book written by a woman whose mother was and is a hoarder. My friend knows that I have a sister who is a hoarder. My mother had those tendencies. So, do I.

What's the definition of a hoarder? Author, Jessie Sholl, says hoarding was defined by two American doctors in 1996 as "the acquisition of, and failure to discard, possessions that are useless or of limited value, resulting in clutter that renders living spaces unusable and causes significant distress and impairment."

Yep. That would be it.

I attribute my sister's condition to her manic need to accumulate and control as well as her compulsive attention to detail... magazines with recipes she'll clip someday, paper documents from five years ago, receipts, unopened mail. It all just piles up. She loves cats, which adds to the chaos.

In her book, *"Dirty Secret: A Daughter Comes Clean about her Mother's Compulsive Hoarding,"* Sholl describes a house crammed to the point that she could not walk around inside. Dirty with unwashed dishes, food, cat boxes piled around.

Another story comes to mind. After many years of trying to help my sister declutter but getting a lot of resistance, she once agreed to let me work on her kitchen. It pretty much matched the description of Sholl's mother's kitchen. Spoiling food, dirty dishes, clutter, garbage to the point that the kitchen was unusable. I filled a couple of big black trash bags with stuff...trash, used paper plates. I got the dishes washed and finally could see the floor to wash it. It had been untouched for several years and was sticky and gritty from filth.

My sister began going through the things I'd put in the trash bags and came across a little pink plastic cup. Something you'd throw away at a party. She went into a rage, shouting at me that "this was the last connection she had with our father from when he was in the hospital." She took the cup out of the bag and put it back on the counter.

God, I thought! I was told that I could not be trusted to clean in her house.

That was the last time that I did.

Like the book author, it was a relief to not care anymore. To not go there.

PATHOLOGICAL HOARDING

The clutter described by Sholl is pathologic. It is crazy stuff except the person is living a rather normal life on the outside. From seeing my sister out and about, friends would never know about the unseen chaos at home.

Maybe it has something to do with inner turmoil. I don't know. It's nearly impossible to help. An offer to clean is viewed as a threat. It was very hard for my sister to let me move anything, throw anything away.

What's happened to her house now that she's living on the farm that she inherited from our mother is anyone's guess. The last time I was there it was chaotic.

A friend joked..."Maybe she should put up a sign up that says, 'This house is full.'"

In a review, People magazine explained that "Sholl explores the psychological reasons why being "merely a pack rat can erupt into full-blown hoarding."

By the end you're sympathetic to both mother and daughter and understand how a parent's obsession can become a child's torment. I am sympathetic to my sister's condition. I do wonder what will happen to her. The last time I was inside mom's farm house, now my sister's, was rapidly being trashed.

Sholl's book reveals that many families struggle with a hoarder. Her memoir published by Simon and Schuster, "is a window into a world that is, at once, strange and strangely familiar." Hoarding has been recognized in children as young as three.

It is thought to affect up to 2 percent of the population but from what I know that estimate could be on the low side.

ALMOST EVERYONE HAS A STORY

And while it is often held at arm's length (hoarders dismissed as "crazy cat ladies", for instance) traces of such behavior are common, wrote book reviewer, Kira Cochrane.

"Almost everyone "seems to have a story, from a friend whose uncle's house was too messy to enter to another whose grandmother kept everything, right down to a bulging bin bag labelled "pieces of string too short for practical use."

I look for signs of hoarding in myself....and I admit that I have tendencies. Most of the storage space in my house if full. I must work to not let my desk pile up, magazines pile up, books pile up while old clothes and shoes linger too long in my closet.

The garage is worse with bags of seed, garden things jamming up corners.

Hoarding is scary. The hoarder is not really coping, but no one can do anything about it. They need support of their families but that's hard when they push you away and seem oblivious to the way they are not coping.

Researchers say that hoarding has something to do with obsessive-compulsive behavior and depression. Hoarders have difficulty making decisions and assign too much value to their possessions making it nearly impossible to get rid of them.

Both psychotherapy and medication may be necessary to treat hoarding, reports the Mayo Clinic. If you have a family member who is a hoarder help them recognize that they have a problem and that they should seek help.

Encourage them to:

– Stick to their treatment plan, try to keep up personal hygiene and bathing and to eat properly.
– Encourage them to reach out to others.
– Remind them that they don't have to live in chaos and distress, they deserve better.

With a professional help, they can take one small step at a time. If they have pets, remind them that they, too, deserve happy and healthy lives with proper nutrition, sanitation and vet care. Most importantly, your hoarder must be able to accept assistance, the Mayo experts said.

FOR MORE:
hoarders.org
hoardingcleanup.com
"The Secret Lives of Hoarders," by Matt Paxton
"Stuff: Compulsive hoarding and the meaning of Things," by
    Gail Steketee
"Digging Out: Helping your loved one manage clutter,
    hoarding, and compulsive acquiring," by Michael Tompkins.

OUR FEET: THINGS HAPPEN, THEY GET BIGGER

"Keep your eyes on the stars,
and your feet on the ground."

-- Theodore Roosevelt, American president, (1858-1919)

FOOT FACTS IN OUR 60s:

- Feet widen as we age. Make sure to measure your feet when buying new shoes.
- Diabetes and peripheral artery disease can cause poor blood flow to the feet.
- Hammertoe is caused by a shortening of the tendons that control toe movement.
- There is no cure for toe nail fungus.
- Toenails become thicker and more brittle with age.
- Good shoes are essential in slowing aging in feet.
- Women seem to have more foot ailments than men.

FIXING FOOT PAIN:

- Lose weight. Take the load off your feet (and knees).
- Check your foot size. Get a comfortable fit.
- Buy good shoes. Feet benefit from more protection and better fit.
- Adjust your workout routine to include lower-impact cardio-exercise.
- If you are experiencing foot pain, see a specialist right away.
- Keep your feet clean and dry. They will thank you.
-

DEFINITIONS:

Podiatrist: A doctor of podiatric medicine (DPM) is qualified to diagnose and treat conditions affecting the foot, ankle, and related structures of the leg. Podiatrists receive medical education and training comparable to medical doctors, including four years of graduate education at one of nine podiatric medical colleges and two or three years of hospital-based residency training.

Orthopedic Surgeon: A medical doctor specializing in orthopedics, a branch of surgery concerned with conditions involving the musculoskeletal system including feet. Orthopedic surgeons complete four years of medical school then five years of residency training in orthopedic surgery.

By the time we reach age 50, experts say our feet have walked about 75,000 miles ---that's more than three times around the earth.

If we're runners, like I have been, some of those miles have been on hard surfaces. And for the sake of style, many of us wore pointy high-heeled shoes to the office every day.

That's a lot of foot torture, say podiatrists and orthopedic surgeons who deal with women's foot problems ranging from aching heel pain and bunions to hammer toes and infections.

By the time we reach 50 and certainly by 60, even if we are healthy and are not over-weight, our feet may begin to complain. If in addition to aging issues, we also face chronic conditions such as diabetes or obesity, then our feet (and knees) can give us real trouble.

Feet are a regular topic of conversation among my friends. Two have had foot surgery to alleviate pain. The good news is that active older women are seeking treatment before the pain causes them to lose mobility. And new technologies are allowing faster recovery from foot surgery and other treatments.

At age 67, I had my feet measured at a store. No surprise, they were a size larger than 10 years earlier.

Maybe it's time to switch from jogging to spinning... or something with less impact.

Dr. Chris Coop, a podiatrist in practice in Vancouver, Wash. for 14 years, emphasizes the importance of preventive care for our feet.

"As we age, our feet are changing, getting longer, flatter and wider," Coop said. "Poor fitting footwear is the No. 1 thing I see contributing to foot pain."

For example, Coop said, people who wear flip-flops to the mall for hours of shopping are more likely to experience these negative results. Poor-fitting high heels that crowd the toes, is another culprit.

WHY WOMEN HAVE MORE FOOT PROBLEMS

Women tend to have more foot problems than men for several reasons, the greatest being that they buy shoes for style, not comfort. In addition, women are more likely to develop certain conditions, such as bunions, which may be inherited.

According to the **American Podiatric Medical Association,** 77 percent of all adults said they had experienced a foot ailment. The number may be higher for women who more often lose elasticity in their foot tendons and ligaments as they age.

Dr. Nancy Kaplan, a podiatrist who works at Sutter Regional Medical Foundation, in Fairfield, Calif. Says women over 50 must shift their shoe wear.

"I tell them that it's OK to spend $100 or $150 on a pair of good shoes," Kaplan said. "Our feet get tired. We never used to live this long or walk these many miles on concrete."

With more baby boomers aging into their 60s and 70s, the world has never seen such a high population of seniors, Kaplan noted.

"That's a lot of aching feet," she said. "We're going to see more and more medical techniques and treatments for feet revolving around that."

Foot ailments to guard against are:

- Plantar fasciitis: Painful inflammation of the connective tissue on the sole of the foot.
- Arthritis in the big toe joint: Painful, achy condition.
- Bunion: Foot deformity caused by an enlargement of the bone and tissue around the joint of the big toe.

- Diabetic foot infection: A complication from numbness and/or poor circulation.

- Diabetic neuropathy: Burning pain in the foot resulting from diabetic condition.

- Hammer toe: A deformity where one or more small toes buckle or bend-under out of their normal position.

- Toe nail fungus: One in five Americans has fungus under the toe nail that causes discoloration and thickening of the nails. Can be a problem and rarely cured.

- Athlete's Foot: Common foot infection that creates itching, scaling and red skin.

FOR MORE:

American Podiatric Medical Association – www.apma.org

American Diabetes Association: Foot Complications – www.diabetes.org

18 Things Your Feet say about Your Health – http://health.yahoo.net

How to Self-Examine Your Feet – gavilanfootcare.com

Top 10 Foot Problems & Treatments – aestheticsinpodiatry.com

Julia Anderson

HEARING AIDS:
MAKING THE RIGHT INVESTMENT

"Deafness is a much worse misfortune (than blindness).
For it means the loss of the most vital stimulus-- the
sound of the voice that brings language, sets thoughts
astir, and keeps us in the intellectual company of man."

-- Helen Keller, the first blind-deaf person to earn a
Bachelor of Arts degree. (1880-1968)

HEARING LOSS FACTS:

Americans with some level of hearing impairment:
37 million

Hearing loss in the total population: 12.1 percent

Hearing loss among adults, 65 and older: 29 percent

Causes of hearing loss: noise, 33 percent; aging, 28 percent; infection or injury, 17 percent; loss at birth, 4.4 percent.

Hearing loss is the third most common health problem in the U.S.

Source: CDC, Atlanta, Ga., Gallaudet Research Institute, Washington D.C.

TYPES OF HEARING LOSS:

Conductive hearing loss: Caused by something that stops sounds from getting through the outer or middle ear. Often can be treated with medicine or surgery.

Sensorineural hearing loss: Occurs when there is a problem with the inner ear or hearing nerve.

Do you regularly ask people to repeat themselves? Does your spouse complain that the sound on the television is too loud? Do you hear crackling noises? Do you hand the phone to someone else when you get a call?

These are signs of hearing loss. Join the club. Nearly 12 percent of all Americans and 30 percent of those 65 and older have trouble hearing.

The good news is that advances in technology are making hearing aids smaller and more effective. Newer models now offer Bluetooth technology that allow you to hear telephone conversions and television audio directly into your hearing aids! The bad news is costs are not coming down and Medicare doesn't cover the expense, which typically can range from $750 per hearing aid to over $3,500.

A national study shows that hearing loss in older people may exacerbate frailty, cognitive decline and other serious medical conditions. The study reported in JAMA Internal Medicine found that annual rates of cognitive decline were 41 percent greater in older adults with hearing problems than in those without.

Women in their 60s are typically shopping for hearing aids for their 90-something mothers. But one day, we may be in the market ourselves, thanks to all that rock and roll.

Addressing hearing loss, however, is about more than buying a hearing aid to amplify sound, said Brad Edgerton, PhD audiologist and director of audiology for Ear, Nose and Throat Clinic of the Northwest in Vancouver, Wash.

"Hearing loss is a tough problem for a lot of people because it's complicated and involves their social structure, their family," Edgerton said. "It's all about how you apply the technology to make life easier and better for people."

COSMETIC ISSUES

Edgerton with 35 years of experience agrees that some patients resist hearing aids for simple cosmetic reasons because they "make them look old."

"My impression is that cosmetics is always important even though attitudes are changing," he said. "There used to be a real stigma with hearing aids because only older folks needed them," he said. "As the technology has gotten smaller, younger people are more willing to explore hearing aids. We now see as many people under age 65 as are over that age."

Miniaturization related to digital computer-chip technology continues to bring changes and improvements to the hearing aid industry. Some digital devices now feature Bluetooth software that allows receiver-in-canal connectivity to smart phones or televisions. For example, someone with hearing loss can enjoy direct amplification from the TV while their spouse and family hear the sound at normal levels.

Even with these advances, no hearing aid can completely restore normal hearing, experts say. The best that can be expected is improved hearing that requires commitment on the part of the patient to manage the device and embrace professional support.

"We try to get a happy customer who will use their hearing aid seven days a week," Edgerton said. "If it's in a drawer unused, it's been a failure."

COSTS ARE DAUNTING

Medicare will cover a hearing medical exam and an audiologist's test if ordered by a physician. Some private Medicare Advantage plans may cover part of hearing aid costs.

Hearing aids are sold with a multitude of brand names, but the reality is that they all are produced by a few manufacturers, among them Starkey, Siemens, Phonak and Microtech. Consumer Reports describes the market as "fragmented and confusing" where consumers face "difficulty sorting out good hearing-aid providers from the less-capable ones."

Prices of hearing aids remain high because research and development costs related to digital technology are increasing. In fact, development and manufacturing costs have risen faster than global demand for hearing aids. Wholesale prices have doubled.

Meanwhile, high prices, mediocre fittings and lack of product information about what they were buying makes the experience less than satisfactory for many, said Consumer Reports.

The magazine's writers said the most important decision when buying hearing aids was to "find the proper professional from whom to buy because it's likely going to be a long-term relationship" with follow-up fittings and device upgrades.

LOANS AND LOW-COST DEALS

If a loan is part of the purchase agreement, make sure you know what you're signing. Some may claim no interest for 12 months but 14 percent interest on a three-year loan.

Financial assistance for low-income clients may be available.

Lions Club International operates the Lions Affordable Hearing Aid Project. The Starkey Hearing Foundation may be another option. Sertoma provides mostly refurbished hearing aids to people who need assistance and state Medicaid programs also may provide hearing aids to people of very limited means.

Contact your local social services agency for an appointment to determine your eligibility for Medicaid. If you're a veteran, seek assistance through the Veterans Administration. Ask your doctor for help in finding low-cost ways to buy hearing aids.

HEARING AID TIPS:

- **Get a check-up.** Before shopping for hearing aids, see an ear, nose and throat physician or a trained audiologist for a hearing test and medical exam. An accurate diagnosis of your problem is essential in selecting the best hearing aid. Some people don't need hearing aids.

- **Look at follow-up service provided by the vendor.** Service is a big part of what you're buying. Check for a warranty on any hearing-aid you might buy.

- **Ask for a trial period.** If a device doesn't meet your needs return it. Be aware of misleading sales tactics -- hearing aids cannot restore normal hearing.

- **Involve spouse and family members in** buying and learning to use a hearing aid. Classes may be available.

- **Price is secondary.** The most expensive device may not be the best for your needs.

- **Don't be afraid of new technology.** Try it and find out what it will do. At the fitting visit, practice talking on the phone and other activities.

- **Be honest with yourself.** Wearing a hearing aid is much less noticeable than asking people to repeat themselves.

- **Shop and compare.**

QUESTIONS WHEN BUYING:

- Does the device have suppression feedback?

- Does the device have directional microphones, which help with conversations in noisy situations or when watching TV?

- Is the device Bluetooth capable? Bluetooth devices can be set to receive direct reception from cells phones and TVs.

- What does the warranty and return policy look like?

- Will follow-up services be available? How many fittings are allowed with the purchase? What's the return policy?

- Make sure office hours and location are convenient. Does the office handle walk-in repairs rather than by appointment?

FOR MORE:
consumerreports.org
audiology.org
betterhearing.org
hearusa.com
aarp.org
disabled-world.com
aidright.com
healthyhearing.com

When You Can't Manage On Your Own

"Be careful to leave your sons well instructed rather than rich, for the hopes of the instructed are better than the wealth of the ignorant."

-- Epictetus, Greek philosopher. (55-135 AD.)

LET'S HAVE A 'MONEY SUMMIT': MAKE A PLAN. TELL YOUR FAMILY.

Financial advisers recommend that families regularly hold "money-summits" to keep everyone in the loop on estate plans, wills and financial decisions. Once a tool of the ultra-wealthy, the family money meeting is now used by families of all economic levels, financial adviser Gordon Bernhardt, says.

This assumes that the people in your family are getting along, are reasonable and can listen to each other without interrupting.

If the people in your family don't fit this "normal" profile, then this post may not be helpful. Although you can find tips below that may give you a strategy for handling difficult family members.

The point here is that holiday family gatherings can be a time for good food, football and for (drum roll please) talking about money. **Just don't do it at the dinner table after everyone has had a few drinks.**

You might ask, why ruin a perfectly good family get-together by bringing up financial matters? Eventually, every family has the conversation. It just might not happen at a very good time, say when there's an emergency because of a catastrophic illness or accident, or somebody's funeral when family members turn to each other with blank looks because nobody knows where the will is or what the person's wishes are when it comes to health care or asset distribution or who is in charge.

Good estate planning includes all family members. That means talking about it. But while everybody thinks these

271

discussions are important, few have the conversations. Why? Because money is a touchy subject, people are afraid of offending each other by bringing up issues and some family members may be competing for influence for how the discussion goes, writes Robyn Post for Money.com. in a post *"How Families Can Talk About Money over Thanksgiving."*

But parents who are still in charge of their finances and estate planning should talk to their kids and even grandkids about where their wills are, who might be assigned power of attorney when they become incapacitated and how assets (including cars, jewelry and furniture) will be distributed when they die or move to a care center.

A big issue for baby boomers may be how to manage grandma, who at 90-something can no longer care for herself.

Even when there's not much net worth, a chat regarding tangible assets should be considered. Tangible assets such as uncle George's clock, the handmade quilts from a great-great-grandmother or uncle Pete's car and savings account, may be worth talking about. Family get-togethers offer an opportunity to have the conversation.

HOW DO YOU BRING IT UP?

There are do's and don'ts, experts say.

Don't bring up money matters or inheritance issues at the holiday dinner table after everyone has had a few drinks. That may not go so well. Instead, let everyone know ahead of time that you'd like to talk about family money matters some time during the get-together.

Set a time that's convenient for everyone...after breakfast first thing; the day after the holiday or the afternoon before the family socializing starts. If you'd rather, have the money-summit as part of a family vacation or get-away some other time.

"Discussing your will and estate planning needs can be a tough topic because it requires coming to terms with mortality," say advisers at Fidelity Investments. Your plans may stir reactions from some of your heirs. But a will and a financial plan also can lower the stress and give everyone (including you) peace of mind.

My ex-parents-in-law, who both died in their 90s, held regular money summits with their two sons during holiday gatherings. The meetings were behind closed doors, separate from any socializing or meals. No wives, no girlfriends, no grandchildren. It was about managing their assets while they were alive and how they would be distributed when they died. Planning went well.

My mother on the other hand struggled to remain in control but left herself open to bullying until (in her 90s), she turned her asset management over to a bank trust department.

Barton Goldsmith writing for Psychology Today offers these tips:

- **Keep your family meeting upbeat**. You might begin with a light-hearted story or two. Ask for family remembrances from those attending. A family meeting is about communication, which can lead to better connections between family members. If you keep the conversation light, it makes the communication easier.

- **Decide who you want in the meeting.** Probably more inclusive is better than, not. Feelings can be hurt. There can be resentment. Every family is unique so plan a careful and thoughtful strategy.

- **Be creative with the meeting space.** It could be a back yard, or a park. Go out. Maybe there's a restaurant with a private space. Avoid the holiday dinner table.

- **Be flexible with the agenda.** Ask those attending to talk about what's been happening in their own worlds. Ask about their future. Start off easy.

- **Consider one-on-one chats.**

Ideally, before the first meeting you meet with each family member separately to hear their issues, give them a chance to talk one-on-one. Then put together a short agenda. First question...what would you like to accomplish as a family in the coming year, next year? Hold these meetings regularly.... twice a year or more, so everyone gets used to the format and the goals.

All of this assumes that families are not having troubles, that there are no dysfunctional family members who dominate discussions, who become emotional or angry, who have an abuse problem, or who face financial challenges?

If that's the case, then careful planning is needed. Or you may decide the holidays may not be the best time. A one-on-one conversation with each family member may be the only thing you do. Or lay out clear ground rules for the discussion.

"Waiting until the holidays to tackle every money skeleton knocking around in your family's closet may wind up putting you through a lot more stress than necessary," say writers at longliveyourmoney.com, a bank-sponsored website. "If time is on your side and you'd like to be more involved in the family's financial planning then why not use the holidays to decide on a recurring time when you can meet throughout the year to check in on one another," they suggest.

WHY ARE THESE CONVERSATIONS WORTH THE EFFORT?

Families need to plan. There's nothing worse than not talking about money, not talking about who you see handling your finances when you no longer can do it yourself. Surprises can leave bitter feelings that destroy relationships.

This is heavy duty stuff. It gets more complicated and harder to do the longer issues are ignored.

Your children may be more likely to understand your planned distribution of property if they hear the motive behind your decisions directly from you, say Fidelity experts. Your children may have good ideas and opinions that can improve your plan. Talking about estate planning allows you to control how our children learn about your decisions....one-on-one or in a family conference.

FIRST STEPS BEFORE A MEETING

Write a will, designate who will have power of attorney if you need help. Final wishes are also important. Those spell out your burial or cremation desires and what you want in a memorial or funeral service.

Things to consider: Setting up a trust to protect assets and ease the distribution process. Determining a charitable giving strategy.

Writing a will outlines how you want your property distributed at your death or who will be your personal representative of your estate. A will provides for paying costs incurred in settling your estate. There are many resources available to help with family estate planning through brokerage firms, at bank trust departments and certainly online.

FOR MORE:
12 Simple Steps to an Estate Plan, nolo.com
How to create a bulletproof estate plan, consumerreports.org
10 Steps to Painless Estate Planning, time.com/money
Health care directives: Taking charge in our later years,
    sixtyandsingle.com

Julia Anderson

FINANCIAL FRAUD:
WHY OUR AGING BRAINS ARE VULNERABLE

"This is devastating...he believed that Rachel was helping him. She created a dream state and kept him there."

-- Brett Hall, attorney for Ralph Raines Jr.
quoted in Willamette Week (Portland, Ore.)

Willamette Week in Portland, Ore., does a darn good job of supplying its readers with edgy news. In an article, *"A Fortune Felled"* writer Kate Willson tells the story of Ralph Raines Jr. who lost his timber-family fortune to a pack of scammers through what investigators call "sweetheart fraud."

The fraudsters, a mother and daughter plus other co-conspirators, stole between $12 million and $20 million from Raines (and his 80-something father) over several years after "befriending" them. Arrests came thanks to an anonymous tip. But by then most of the money had gone into new cars including a $200,000 Ferrari, lavish trips to Las Vegas, rental property purchases and, as they say, thin air.

The story is all too familiar (see posts at sixtyandsingle.com on elder abuse) and raises these questions: What happens to our brains when we get old and why do we lose reasoning capacity that protected us from scammers when we're younger?

Financial predators show up in many forms. They can be aggressive investment brokers who make a commission every time they sell an annuity or churn an account, or they can be caretakers who begin by paying your bills but are soon tapping checking accounts and selling your house.

Having watched my mother age over the final 20 years of her life, I'd say she began to lose it in her mid-80s when two separate brokers sold her annuities, one at $50,000, the other $40,000. In both cases, when questioned later, she could not explain why either annuity would benefit her or her heirs. They didn't.

Meanwhile, both financial advisers earned hefty up-front commissions on the sales.

Not long after that, my sister coerced my mother out of $10,000 to finance a poorly thought-out wrongful firing lawsuit. Of course, the case went nowhere.

My mother was not senile in any obvious way. She sincerely believed that she could still manage. With most things such as re-upping a CD investment, she did. Only when pressured did she slip up and give in.

In her 90s she sought the help of a bank trust to manage all her assets -- a productive farm and her investments. That allowed her to live her final years in relative peace and financial security at the care center with the bank trust in charge of her money and paying her bills.

Research shows that older women such as my mother are nearly twice as likely to become victims of financial abuse as men. That is frankly because men die earlier, and women are left to fend for themselves. Family members, friends or neighbors are usually the financial abusers.

My mother's slip-ups were small compared to the Raines' story. But every day, everywhere, elderly people are putting their trust in someone who may see them only as a meal ticket, if not a free trip to Vegas.

WHAT HAPPENS TO OUR BRAINS?

Neuroscientific and psychological research shows that as people age "they become more focused on maximizing positive emotions and social interactions," reports Jason Zweig in a Wall Street Journal article. "Older people become more determined to block out negative experiences. This leads older people to pay more attention to those who make them feel content and comfortable."

In the Raines case, when investigators confronted him with the harsh facts of his financial abuse, he denied at first that there was a problem and refused to believe he'd been duped.

Wanting to feel positive about those around us as we age is not the only challenge, researchers say.

Our cognitive abilities begin to slip as we move into our 70s and 80s. Older investors, for instance, tend to make simple errors that younger investors would avoid, wrote Zweig.

It may be particularly difficult for those who have made sensible financial decisions throughout their lives to in old age come to terms with a decline in their reasoning capacity. These people may continue to feel confident even as they begin to lose it.

LOSING CAPACITY

Robert Willis, an economist and professor at the University of Michigan, has made a study of financial decision-making among the elderly. In a workshop, Willis points out that we face a *"growing complexity of decisions"* related to old age. Everything from medicines people take to health care insurance decisions is more complex. Never mind investment decisions and asset management.

"While people accumulate financial knowledge and skills over their lifetime, at older ages they confront the serious risk of losing these capacities if they acquire Alzheimer's disease or other types of dementia that causes progressive declines in cognition and eventual complete loss of functional capacities," Willis writes.

"This may pose an enormous financial risk to all members of a household."

FINANCIALLY VULNERABLE

Forgetting to pay bills is minor compared with being duped in fraudulent schemes or signing contracts that we don't understand.

"Regardless of cognitive status, older American are more financially vulnerable than the general population," Willis underscores in *"The Implications of Alzheimer's Risk for Household Financial Decision-making,"* co-written with Joanne Hsu of the Federal Reserve Board.

How can we gracefully manage our decline into happy old age, free of confusion and/or financial abuse? The trick is putting a plan in place before that time comes. Who or what organization will manage your assets when you get really old? And how do you avoid being scammed?

TIPS FROM THE U.S. DEPARTMENT OF LABOR:

Don't let fear, desperation, or the need to catch up financially push you (or family members) into any hasty investment decisions. In all legitimate investments, higher returns are accompanied by higher risks - risks you may well not want to take as you near retirement. Be wary of anyone who claims they can sell you a product that offers great reward without great risk - a sure sign of a scam.

Recognize that anyone can claim to be a "financial consultant" or "investment counselor." That person may not have the special training, expertise, or credentials necessary to back up the claim. Ask about licensing and professional designations and check them out with securities regulators and any trade groups in which they claim membership.

Understand your investments and never be afraid to ask questions. Good financial professionals are never pushy, and they never dismiss your concerns.

Don't let embarrassment or fear keep you from reporting suspected investment fraud or abuse.

Never judge a person's integrity by how they sound or how they appear. The most successful con artists sound extremely professional and can make even the flimsiest investment seem as safe as putting money in the bank.

Monitor your investments. Ask tough questions and insist on speedy and satisfactory answers. Make sure you get regular written and oral reports

My advice: Use a bank trust department. Banks are bound by law to take a conservative and professional approach to their customer's money. They must send you a monthly financial report showing income and outgo. For a small fee, which should be less than 1 percent of total assets, a bank trust manager is there to be a gatekeeper, to make sure you can live comfortably and happily in your old age. The challenge is deciding when you should no longer be in charge.

Baby boomers would do well to set up a simple plan and stick with it, as recommended by Laura Carstensen, director of the **Stanford Center on Longevity.** A TEDTalk presenter and the author of several books and articles including, ***"Growing Old or Living Long: Take Your Pick,"*** Carstensen says we cannot regret growing older.

"Old age is still perceived as a period of sadness by young people and older people themselves, even though most older people (in recent studies) describe themselves as quite satisfied," Carstensen said. "Contrary to the popular view that youth is the best time of life, the peak of emotional life may not occur until well into the seventh decade."

Therefore, we must plan for the time when we may not have quite the investment savvy we had in our 60s. Ralph Raines Jr. certainly had no plan or had anyone (family or friend) close enough to provide honest financial advice. Instead he turned to scammers who made him happy and comfortable as they stole his fortune.

FOR MORE:
National Council on Aging, "22 tips for avoiding scams and swindles."
National Center on Elder Abuse
National Institute of Justice, Financial Exploitation of the Elderly
"Would Your Adult Children Rip You Off?" · Bankrate.com
"Why Everything You Think about Aging May be Wrong," Wall Street Journal

DYING TOO LATE: WHAT WORRIES US
ABOUT END-OF-LIFE CARE

"Medical overtreatment costs the U.S. health care system
an estimated $158 billion to $226 billion a year.
About $550 billion of Medicare's annual budget pays for
medical treatment in the last year of life."

--Katy Butler from her book, *"Knocking on Heaven's Door:*
The Path to a Better Way of Death."

A photo of my mother when she was in her vital 60s holds a prominent place on my bedroom wall. Hands on hips, she takes a jaunty pose for the camera. That was more than 30 years ago.

My mother was then living on the farm with my father. She had a full life working with charity groups and caring for her aging parents, both in their 90s. They died respectively at ages 93 and 98. My grandmother faded into dementia. My grandfather died from a stroke after lingered in the hospital unconscious on IVs for more than a month.

Mother talked about her father's prolonged ordeal. "When I get that old I'm just going to stop eating," she once said.

In her final years at the care center, she tipped over once getting out of a chair. After five hours of observation and despite my mother repeatedly saying she did NOT want to go to the hospital, the night crew called paramedics who carted her to the ER at 10 o'clock that night.

She was kept awake while technicians ran her through an MRI machine, did x-rays and then stuck her in a hospital bed on an IV, which leaked into her arm causing a huge bruise.

It took her two days to get out after a "hospitalist" said she was fine and sent her back to the care center. The total cost of this episode was somewhere north of $10,000. Medicare and additional insurance covered most of the expense. Mother hated every minute of the experience.

It took days to get her strength back. She now has signed Advanced Care/Scope of Treatment directives posted in her room saying that in a medical emergency, she is to be made comfortable and remain at the care center, unless she is in serious pain. In the end, my mother had one final stroke and died at 98 with the support of hospice.

Author Katy Butler has written about end-of-life health care decisions in her book, *"Knocking on Heaven's Door: The Path to a Better Way of Death."* In a Wall Street Journal excerpt, Butler describes her 85-year-old mother's decision to forgo heart-valve surgery and instead remain at home, facing death with the help of hospice. "She died well because she was willing to die too soon rather than too late," wrote Butler.

My mother lived enthusiastically engaged in the moment. She wanted to die well on her own terms without the help of the plugged-in American health care system. She did, but it was a fight.

FOR MORE:

"Best Care May Be Dying Well," - Janice Lloyd, USA TODAY.

"Dying Well in America: What is Required of Physicians?" by Richard Payne, M.D.

"Dying in America," The National Academies of Sciences, nationalacademies.org

DyingWell.org, Dr. Ira Byock, M.D.

---

6 STEPS TO TAKE CHARGE
AT THE END OF YOUR LIFE

*"A dying man needs to die, as a sleepy man needs to
sleep, and there comes a time when it is wrong,
as well as useless, to resist."*

-- Stewart Alsop, newspaper columnist. (1914-1974)

Those who have watched their parents slip into old age
then face multiple health challenges before passing
through death's door, know that the end-of-life journey can be
tricky.

Modern medicine has made old age more possible, even more
tolerable than in generations past. The tricky part is how we plan
for these last years.

Legal documents called advanced health care directives -- a
living will, do-not-resuscitate instructions and designation of
(health care) power of attorney – can smooth the way for ourselves
and our families.

But lately, questions have arisen about how well patients,
their families, doctors and other caregivers understand advanced
health care directives. The Institute of Medicine and the National
Academy of Sciences are calling for improvements in both medical
and social services end-of-life care.

A massive report, *"Dying in America,"* cites these issues: A
lack of awareness or interest by both patients and their families
in completing advance directive forms. Lack of institutional

support for completing advance directives. Clinicians' unwillingness to adhere to patients' wishes, resistance within the medical culture and differences in families' culture traditions for completing health care directives.

Despite these challenges, we can do a lot to ensure that our own end of life care is as comfortable and meaningful as possible. Here's how:

1. Accept that fully 70 percent of us who become critically ill at the end of our lives will be incapable of participating in decisions about our health care. Without advance health care directives, we might find ourselves in a hospital intensive care unit under the eye of an "intensivist physician" whose only job is to keep us alive at whatever cost -- physical, emotional and financial.

2. Write a will and create a "living will" outlining the kind of care you wish to receive if you are no longer competent or in a vegetative state. Appoint a legal health care representative to carry out your wishes.

3. Write a Do-Not-Resuscitate directive which tells any caregivers – doctors, emergency personnel – to not intervene if you have no pulse or are not breathing. You can wear a DNR bracelet or get a tattoo. Even a tattoo didn't work in one recent emergency room case.

4. Make it clear to all family members that there will be no heroics. Get your legal directives filed with your doctor, the fire department and all family members. If you go into a care facility, have the DNR posted in BIG TYPE in plain sight in your room. (Even that measure didn't prevent a trip to the ER in the year before my mother died at age 98). Only post contact information for your legal health care representative at your care center door. Keep other family member numbers elsewhere, so there is no confusion over who staff should call in an emergency.

5. Tell your "friends" at the care center to not call 911 if you have a health crisis. Remember that if 911 gets involved, all the legally signed requests go out the window. The emergency

folks are bound to preserve life...no matter what. The same goes for doctors in emergency rooms. (A huge brouhaha in California not long ago created industry turmoil when a bystander called 911 after a fellow care center resident had a stroke but the nursing staff (citing her wishes) did not provide aid.

6. Legally assign someone with durable power of attorney to manage your financial affairs and make health care decisions for you when or if you become incompetent or incapacitated. Set up a bank trust that designates you as co-trustee until you hand over management of your financial affairs to the bank. File your legal instructions with your doctor, the fire department, the care center and with all family members. Use legal forms that are state-specific. You can find them at americanbar.org or printable advance directive forms by state from AARP at www.aarp.org.

Most of us wish for a peaceful death in bed at home. The reality is seven out of 10 of us will spend our last years in a care facility.

And even with good planning we likely will find weaknesses in our end-of-life initiatives. Some are outlined in "The Good Death" by Ann Neumann where she writes about the experience of her father's dying. **"Part of the reason we don't know how people die is because we no longer see it up close,"** she writes. "Death has been put off and professionalized to the point where we no longer have to dirty our hands with it."

But we should. We can help ourselves and our loved ones do better by getting our instructions on paper and by talking at length about these issues with our family and our caregivers.

FOR MORE:
"The Good Death," by Ann Neumann.
"Dying in America," from the Institute of Medicine.
"Knocking on Heaven's Door: The Path to a Better Way of Death," by Katy Butler.

Julia Anderson

CONCLUSION:
OUR SIXTIES IN TWO WORDS

When we began monthly coffee get-togethers 12 years ago, 5 women friends and I were in our late 50s and talked mostly about our aging parents and in-laws as they faced end-of-life care issues. Soon they were supporting me though an unwanted and unexpected divorce. We then shared the journey of loss with another whose husband slowly died of Parkinson's disease.

Now, we talk about our children, our own health and about how to be fashionable without looking like we're trying too hard.

You name it, we've lived it --- divorce, death, loss, retirement, widowhood, remarriage and health issues. I asked my friends to sum up the decade of their 60s in two words.

Here is their take!

Pretty scary

Very liberating.

Loving life!

Freaking rollercoaster!

Living free!

It sucks. It rocks!

Freaking fantastic!

More challenging.

Profoundly boring.

Measured optimism.

Great age!

Total Freedom.

Smart Women, Smart Money, Smart Life
ends with this from American author
Nancy Thayer, who said:

"It's never too late – in fiction or in life – to revise."

Julia Anderson

Glossary of Investment Terms

401(k): A contribution plan where employees can make contributions from his or her paycheck either before or after-tax, depending on the options offered in the plan. The money grows tax-free until time of withdrawal. Employers usually offer matching money as an incentive to save for the long-term. Contributions reduce gross taxable income in the year of the contribution

Accumulated Interest. The same compounding works for shares of stock. Dividends are reinvested into more stock.

Annuity: A contractual insurance product that pays out income over time. They can be fixed or variable. It is important to know how both work.

Bond: A fixed income investment in which an investor loans money to an entity with a maturity date for when the principal is repaid plus interest. **(Why bond values go down when interest rates go up**: Rising Interest Rates, make pre-existing bonds decrease in value because to attract demand, the price of the pre-existing bond must drop in price enough to match the same return yielded by new higher prevailing interest rates.)

Certificate of Deposit: A savings certificate with a fixed maturity date, fixed interest rate payment guarantees with a certain minimum deposit requirement

Compound growth/interest: The addition of interest to the principal sum of a loan or deposit. In other words, interest on interest. It is the result of reinvesting interest, rather than paying it out, so that interest in the next period is then earned on the principal sum plus previously

Cost basis: The original value of an asset for tax purposes, usually the purchase price. Cost basis can be applied to stock, real estate or other investment.

Dividend: A sum of money paid regularly (usually quarterly) by a company to its shareholders (stock owners) out of profits or reserves.

Earnings per share: A company's profit divided by its number of common outstanding shares. Can be compared with other publicly traded companies in the same industry.

Expense ratio: The annual fee that all funds charge their shareholders. Expressed as a percentage of assets deducted each fiscal year for fund expenses. Also called management fee, administrative fee or operating costs.

Fixed Income: Income from a pension or investment that is set at a particular figure and does not vary. Generally, refers to bonds.

Individual Retirement Account: A tax-deferred investment tool that allows an individual to save for retirement with tax-free growth. Taxes are paid when money is withdrawn from an IRA. Withdrawals are required at 70 1/2. Contributions reduce gross taxable income in the year of the contribution

Interest Rates (loans vs investments): The percent of principal charged by a lender for the use of its money. (Ex: Mortgage interest rates). Conversely, banks pay interest rates on savings to attract deposits. (CDs offer fixed interest rates)

Managed accounts/funds: A fee-based investment product such as a mutual fund or customized portfolio managed by a professional money manager.

Mutual fund: Pooled money from many investors that trades in diversified holdings (stocks, bonds, real estate or other) and is professionally managed.

P/E ratio: The measure of the share price relative to the annual net income earned by a firm. The PE ratio shows current demand for a company share.

Publicly traded company: A corporation whose ownership is dispersed among the public in many shares of stock, which are freely traded on markets.

Roth IRA: A tax-free retirement savings tool using after-tax dollars. While a Roth gives no tax deduction on the front end, the growth and the eventual withdrawals are federal TAX-FREE.

Stock: The stock (shares) of a corporation traded on stock exchanges.

Share price: The price of a single share of saleable stock shares of a company.

Stock markets: A market where stocks and bonds are bought and sold. Prices are based on corporate earnings. (Also called stock exchanges)

Stock symbol: Or ticker symbol. An abbreviation used to uniquely identify publicly traded shares of a certain stock -- letters, numbers or a combination.

Unrealized gain/loss: An unrealized gain is a profit that exists on paper, resulting from an investment such as a stock. A gain becomes realized once the position is closed (sold) for a profit. Same with unrealized loss.

Smart Money
Video Topics

Search on YouTube for: Smart Money Julia Anderson

Evaluating an employment early buyout
How to hold a family money meeting
What is a reverse mortgage
Preventing elder financial abuse
Social Security myths
Charitable giving in retirement
Social Security – How to maximize retirement income
Why have a will
Traveling with grandchildren
Talking to kids about money
Buying a franchise business in retirement, do's and don'ts
And more...

Julia Anderson

Index

About the author

Julia Anderson is an award-winning personal finance columnist and business news writer with more than 35 years of experience. She hosts the **Smart Money** interview program at public television TVCTV in Beaverton, Ore. Those interviews are available on YouTube by searching Julia Anderson Smart Money. She leads **Own Your Future** "money" workshops to help people financially plan for the long-term.

At 60, Anderson founded **sixtyandsingle.com** where she writes for woman about money, investing and managing life's challenges.

For much of her career, Anderson was the business news editor at **The Columbian** newspaper in Vancouver, Wash. During that tenure, her business news section was named best in the U.S. for medium-size papers. Her columns won numerous **Society of Professional Journalist** awards. She was the Smart Money columnist for the **Portland Tribune** and for eight years was a business news and financial commentator on **KXL 101.1 FM** radio in Portland.

She is married, has two sons and three step-daughters. With her husband, Ken, she enjoys travel, fishing, skiing and rafting on Pacific Northwest rivers. The couple live in Southwest Wash., near Portland, Ore.

Julia Anderson